The United Nations High Commissioner for Refugees (UNHCR)

The United Nations High Commissioner for Refugees (UNHCR) is a concise and comprehensive introduction to both the world of refugees and the organizations that protect and assist them. Written by experts in the field, this is one of the very few books that traces the relationship between state interests, global politics, and the work of the UNHCR. This book will appeal to students, scholars, practitioners, and readers with an interest in international relations. Key topics discussed include:

- UNHCR as an actor in world politics since 1950
- the refugee definition and protection instruments
- institutional strengths and weaknesses
- asylum crises in the global north and global south
- protracted refugee situations and internally displaced persons
- key criticisms and the continuing relevance of UNHCR

Gil Loescher is Visiting Professor, Refugee Studies Centre, and Senior Research Associate, Centre for International Studies at the University of Oxford, and Emeritus Professor of Political Science at the University of Notre Dame, Indiana. He is the author of several books on refugees and international relations, including *The UNHCR and World Politics*.

Alexander Betts is Hedley Bull Research Fellow in International Relations at the University of Oxford, where he is Director of the MacArthur Foundation-funded Global Migration Governance project. He has worked at UNHCR headquarters and is author of the forthcoming book *North-South Impasse: the International Politics of Refugee Protection*.

James Milner is Postdoctoral Fellow at the Munk Centre for International Studies, University of Toronto, and will be Assistant Professor of Political Science, Carleton University, from summer 2008. He has worked with UNHCR in headquarters and the field, and is the author of the forthcoming book *Refugees, the State and the Politics of Asylum in Africa*.

Routledge Global Institutions

Edited by Thomas G. Weiss
The CUNY Graduate Center, New York, USA
and Rorden Wilkinson
University of Manchester, UK

About the Series

The Global Institutions Series is designed to provide readers with comprehensive, accessible, and informative guides to the history, structure, and activities of key international organizations. Every volume stands on its own as a thorough and insightful treatment of a particular topic, but the series as a whole contributes to a coherent and complementary portrait of the phenomenon of global institutions at the dawn of the millennium.

Books are written by recognized experts, conform to a similar structure, and cover a range of themes and debates common to the series. These areas of shared concern include the general purpose and rationale for organizations, developments over time, membership, structure, decision-making procedures, and key functions. Moreover, current debates are placed in historical perspective alongside informed analysis and critique. Each book also contains an annotated bibliography and guide to electronic information as well as any annexes appropriate to the subject matter at hand.

The volumes currently published or under contract include:

The United Nations and Human Rights (2005)
A guide for a new era
by Julie Mertus (American University)

The UN Secretary General and Secretariat (2005)
by Leon Gordenker (Princeton University)

United Nations Global Conferences (2005)
by Michael G. Schechter (Michigan State University)

The UN General Assembly (2005)
by M.J. Peterson (University of Massachusetts, Amherst)

Internal Displacement (2006)
Conceptualization and its consequences
by Thomas G. Weiss (The CUNY Graduate Center) and David A. Korn

Global Environmental Institutions (2006)
by Elizabeth R. DeSombre (Wellesley College)

African Economic Institutions
by Kwame Akonor (Seton Hall University)

The United Nations Development Programme (UNDP)
by Elizabeth A. Mandeville (Tufts University) and Craig N. Murphy (Wellesley College)

The Regional Development Banks
Lending with a regional flavor
by Jonathan R. Strand (University of Nevada, Las Vegas)

Multilateral Cooperation Against Terrorism
by Peter Romaniuk (John Jay College of Criminal Justice, CUNY)

Transnational Organized Crime
by Frank Madsen (University of Cambridge)

Peacebuilding
From concept to commission
by Robert Jenkins (University of London)

Governing Climate Change
by Peter Newell (University of East Anglia) and Harriet A. Bulkeley (Durham University)

Millennium Development Goals (MDGs)
For a people-centered development agenda?
by Sakiko Fukada-Parr (The New School)

For further information regarding the series, please contact:

Craig Fowlie, Publisher, Politics & International Studies
Taylor & Francis
2 Park Square, Milton Park, Abingdon
Oxford OX14 4RN, UK

+44 (0)207 842 2057 Tel
+44 (0)207 842 2302 Fax

Craig.Fowlie@tandf.co.uk
www.routledge.com

The United Nations High Commissioner for Refugees (UNHCR)

The politics and practice of refugee protection into the twenty-first century

**Gil Loescher,
Alexander Betts,
and James Milner**

Routledge
Taylor & Francis Group

LONDON AND NEW YORK

First published 2008
by Routledge
2 Park Square, Milton Park, Abingdon, Oxon OX14 4RN

Simultaneously published in the USA and Canada
by Routledge
270 Madison Avenue, New York, NY 10016

Routledge is an imprint of the Taylor & Francis Group, *an informa business*

Typeset in Times New Roman by
Taylor & Francis Books
Printed and bound in Great Britain by
MPG Books Ltd, Bodmin

British Library Cataloguing in Publication Data
A catalogue record for this book is available from the British Library

Library of Congress Cataloging in Publication Data
Loescher, Gil.
     UNHCR : the politics and practice of refugee protection into the 21st
century / Gil Loescher, Alexander Betts, James Milner.
        p. cm. – (Routledge global institutions)
     Includes bibliographical references and index.
     [etc.]
     1. Office of the United Nations High Commissioner for Refugees. 2.
     Refugees–Government policy. 3. Refugees–International cooperation. I.
     Betts, Alexander. II. Milner, James. III. Title.
     HV640.3.L634 2008
362.87′56–dc22   2007042494
ISBN 978-0-415-40347-4 (hbk)
ISBN 978-0-415-41863-8 (pbk)
ISBN 978-0-203-92839-4 (ebk)

Contents

Illustrations

Figures

Tables

Foreword

The current volume is the twenty-third in a dynamic series on "global institutions." The series strives (and, based on the volumes published to date, succeeds) to provide readers with definitive guides to the most visible aspects of what many of us know as "global governance." Remarkable as it may seem, there exist relatively few books that offer in-depth treatments of prominent global bodies, processes and associated issues, much less an entire series of concise and complementary volumes. Those that do exist are either out of date, inaccessible to the non-specialist reader, or seek to develop a specialized understanding of particular aspects of an institution or process rather than offer an overall account of its functioning. Similarly, existing books have often been written in highly technical language or have been crafted "in-house" and are notoriously self-serving and narrow.

The advent of electronic media has undoubtedly helped research and teaching by making data and primary documents of international organizations more widely available, but it has also complicated matters. The growing reliance on the Internet and other electronic methods of finding information about key international organizations and processes has served, ironically, to limit the educational and analytical materials to which most readers have ready access—namely, books. Public relations documents, raw data, and loosely refereed web sites do not make for intelligent analysis. Official publications compete with a vast amount of electronically available information, much of which is suspect because of its ideological or self-promoting slant. Paradoxically, a growing range of purportedly independent web sites offering analyses of the activities of particular organizations has emerged, but one inadvertent consequence has been to frustrate access to basic, authoritative, readable, critical, and well-researched texts. The market for such has actually been reduced by the ready availability of varying quality electronic materials.

For those of us who teach, research, and practice in the area, such limited access to information has been particularly frustrating. We were delighted when Routledge saw the value of a series that bucks this trend and provides key reference points to the most significant global institutions and issues. They are betting that serious students and professionals will want serious analyses. We have assembled a first-rate line-up of authors to address that market. Our intention is to provide one-stop shopping for all readers—students (both undergraduate and postgraduate), negotiators, diplomats, practitioners from non-governmental and intergovernmental organizations, and interested parties alike—seeking information about most prominent institutional aspects of global governance.

UNHCR

The most reliable indicator of suffering in war zones is usually the number of "refugees"—that is, in the vernacular or according to the text of the 1951 UN Convention on Refugees, exiles who flee across the borders of their country of origin. Physical displacement is *prima facie* evidence of vulnerability because people who are deprived of their homes and communities and means of livelihood are unable to resort to traditional coping capacities.

When we designed this series, humanitarian issues loomed large for contemporary international relations. So, we wanted to make sure that the two "gold standard" institutions in this field were part of the Global Institutions Series, the International Committee of the Red Cross (ICRC) and the UN High Commissioner for Refugees (UNHCR). In 2006, the volume on ICRC was published,[1] and we are delighted that this essential one on UNHCR is now before our readers. What a pleasure to read such a polished, well-structured, and nicely argued text, and to be able to do so in tandem with the one on the ICRC, another recent book on the difficulties of assisting and protecting internally displaced persons (IDPs), and two books in the series on human rights.[2]

Dealing with the human debris from contemporary wars is anything but straightforward, especially since the so-called new wars of the post-Cold War period. Killing, maiming, raping, and displacing civilians, has become part of the strategy of belligerents. Our era has witnessed the coining of the ugly "ethnic cleansing" and the reality of the "well-fed dead"—people who have been temporarily rescued by international efforts but then are abandoned to their fates afterwards.

As Mrs. Sadako Ogata wrote in her autobiography of a decade as the UN High Commissioner for Refugees: "There are no humanitarian solutions to humanitarian problems."[3] Even temporary solutions require political will and international capacities.

The subtitle of the current volume ensures that these larger issues are integral to an understanding of UNHCR, namely "the politics and practice of refugee protection into the twenty-first century." Indeed, one of the institutional adaptations most challenging for UNHCR has been the challenge of dealing with "people in refugee-like situations." Part of the story here includes UNHCR's efforts to help IDPs and environmental refugees. The former has been especially difficult because UNHCR and other agencies are seeking to help persons who have not crossed a border, which requires permission from the very political authorities who are responsible for the displacement.

Given the complexity of a book on human beings caught in the throes of war, we needed a first-rate scholar with a track record in publishing the very best work in the area. No one knows more or has written more insightfully about international efforts over the years to deal with forced migration than Gil Loescher. So, we were delighted that he took up our challenge and associated two younger colleagues, Alexander Betts and James Milner.

Gil Loescher is Senior Research Fellow at the Centre for International Studies, University of Oxford. He has written so many books, articles, and policy papers on refugees and forced migration that it would be tedious to list more than simply the two most widely cited ones, namely *The UNHCR and World Politics: A Perilous Path* and *Beyond Charity: International Cooperation and the Global Refugee Problem.*[4] Most notably for our purposes, he has been associated as an external advisor for all of the UNHCR's *State of the World's Refugees* and numerous policy and evaluation reports.[5] As for all of the most insightful research on war and its victims, Gil has always felt obliged to move beyond the stacks in libraries to observe first-hand situations on the ground and interview international officials and the people whom they assist and protect. Fortunately, Gil has made a heroic recovery after being one of the casualties of the attack on UN headquarters in Baghdad in August 2003 when twenty-two colleagues died—an inspiration to all those who care about the quality of analysis that improves the quality of assistance and protection.

Joining Loescher as co-authors are two younger scholars who have already established themselves as among the next generation of leading researchers on forced migration and international relations. Betts and Milner both have direct and analytical experience with refugees and UNHCR. In addition to working for UNHCR, Alexander Betts has worked for the Council of Europe and is currently Hedley Bull

Research Fellow in International Relations at the University of Oxford. He has published on international cooperation and the global refugee regime in the *Journal of Refugee Studies, Global Governance,* and UNHCR's "New Issues" Working Paper Series, as well as a chapter in *The State of the World's Refugees.*[6] James Milner has been a consultant for UNHCR in India, Cameroon, Guinea, and at Geneva headquarters, and he has served as an advisor to the UK Home Office and the European Council on Refugees and Exiles. He is currently SSHRC Post-doctoral Fellow at the Munk Centre for International Studies, University of Toronto and has recently co-authored a number of works with Gil Loescher, including *Protracted Refugee Situations: Domestic and International Security Implications* and articles in *International Affairs, Survival,* and the *Journal of Conflict, Development and Security.*[7]

As always, we look forward to comments from first-time or veteran readers of the Global Institutions Series.

Thomas G. Weiss, The CUNY Graduate Center, New York, USA
Rorden Wilkinson, University of Manchester, UK
February 2008

Acknowledgments

The writing of this book has drawn on many years of thinking, teaching and publishing on the subject of refugees and UNHCR. Each of the authors brings different strengths and experiences to this subject. All three of us have had experience working with or for UNHCR either at headquarters or in the field, and this experience has largely shaped our understanding of the organization.

We have also benefited greatly from our discussions with UN staff, particularly those at UNHCR, and with government and NGO representatives over the years. The insights and experiences of these individuals, colleagues and friends have contributed significantly to our understanding of the challenges faced by the refugee regime. In particular, we would like to thank:

Mamadou Dian Balde, Beverley Byfield, Jeff Crisp, Khassim Diagne, Jean-François Durieux, Erika Feller, Bill Frelick, Ichiro Fujisaki, Elissa Golberg, Raymond Hall, Arafat Jamal, Laura Joyce, David Lambo, Brian Lander, Janet Lim, Salvatore Lombardo, Ewen MacLeod, Augustine Mahiga, Dennis McNamara, Kamal Morjane, Sumbul Rizvi, Yasser Saad, Ed Schenkenberg van Mierop, Wegger Strommen, Manisha Thomas, and Hasim Utkan.

We would also thank a number of colleagues and scholars whose writings and presentations have influenced our thinking on UNHCR and the global refugee regime:

Michael Barnett, Michael Barutciski, B.S. Chimni, Matthew Gibney, Anne Hammerstad, Arthur Helton, Andrew Hurrell, Bonaventure Rutinwa, and Nick Van Hear.

The authors are also grateful for the support of the Centre for International Studies, University of Oxford, the Munk Centre for International Studies, University of Toronto, the Ford Foundation, the Rose Research Fellowship at Lady Margaret Hall, Oxford, and the Social Science and Humanities Research Council of Canada.

Despite our close association with UNHCR, this book does not represent an official account of either the history or policies of the Office. We received no financial assistance from the Office for the research or writing of this book. We have tried to write an honest and independent assessment of UNHCR, focusing in particular on the tensions between the organization's normative mission and agenda of protecting and assisting the world's refugees and the problems of implementing these in a world dominated by state interests.

Due to constraints of space our book does not cover all of the refugee emergencies that UNHCR has been involved in over the past half-century. Rather, we have focused on the major developments and policies that have shaped the evolution of UNHCR as an important global actor.

Some of the material in this book draws on the authors' previous writings, in particular Gil Loescher's *The UNHCR and World Politics: A Perilous Path* (Oxford: Oxford University Press, 2001).

We are also grateful to Maria Clara Martin, Head of the Appeals and Reports Unit, Donor Relations and Resource Mobilization Service, UNHCR, for permission to use the illustrations from UNHCR's 2006 Global Appeal.

Abbreviations

1951 Convention	1951 Convention Relating to the Status of Refugees
1967 Protocol	1967 Protocol Relating to the Status of Refugees
4 Rs	repatriation, reintegration, rehabilitation and reconstruction
AU	the African Union
CIREFCA	International Conference on Central American Refugees (1989)
CPA	Comprehensive Plan of Action
DAR	Development Assistance for Refugees
DDR	disarmament, demobilization and reintegration
DHA	United Nations Department of Humanitarian Affairs
DLI	Development through Local Integration
DPKO	Department of Peacekeeping Operations
ECOSOC	Economic and Social Council
EEC	European Economic Community
ERC	Emergency Relief Coordinator
ExCom	Executive Committee of the Programme of the United Nations High Commissioner for Refugees
HSO	Humanitarian Security Officer
IASC	Inter-Agency Standing Committee
ICARA I	First International Conference on Assistance to Refugees in Africa
ICARA II	Second International Conference on Assistance to Refugees in Africa
ICMC	International Catholic Migration Commission
ICRC	International Committee of the Red Cross
ICVA	International Council of Voluntary Agencies
IDP	internally displaced person
IFRC	International Federation of Red Cross and Red Crescent Societies

IGC	Intergovernmental Consultations on Asylum and Migration
ILO	International Labour Organization
IOM	International Organization for Migration
IRC	International Rescue Committee
IRO	International Refugee Organization
ISM	irregular secondary movements
LWF	Lutheran World Federation
MoU	Memorandum of Understanding
NATO	North Atlantic Treaty Organization
NGO	non-governmental organization
OAU	Organization of African Unity
OCHA	Office for the Coordination of Humanitarian Affairs
OSCE	Organization for Security and Cooperation in Europe
PRS	protracted refugee situation
RAD	refugee aid and development
SHAEF	Supreme Headquarters Allied Expeditionary Force
SRV	Socialist Republic of Vietnam
TDA	targeted development assistance
UN	the United Nations
UNDP	United Nations Development Programme
UNDRO	United Nations Disaster Relief Coordinator
UNHCR	United Nations High Commissioner for Refugees
UNICEF	United Nations Children's Fund
UNPROFOR	United Nations Protection Force
UNRRA	United Nations Relief and Rehabilitation Agency
UNSECORD	United Nations Security Coordinator
USCRI US	United States Committee for Refugees and Immigrants
USG	Under-Secretary-General
WFP	World Food Programme

Introduction

There have always been refugees. Wars, political upheavals, ethnic discrimination, religious strife and a wide range of other human rights refugee's abuses lead people to become refugees. (Refugees are people who have definition suffered human rights violations and who have fled across the borders of their home countries to seek protection elsewhere.) Throughout the past century, there have been many peaks and troughs in the overall numbers of refugees and other displaced people in the world, with huge numbers during the two world wars and during the 1980s and 1990s. In mid-2007, the global number of refugees stood at almost 10 million, with another 25 million people internally displaced.

Despite the longstanding historical significance of refugees, it was only in the twentieth century that a formal institutional structure was created to address their needs. Following a number of precedents before and during the Second World War, the Office of the United Nations High Commissioner for Refugees (UNHCR) was created in 1950 to protect refugees and find a solution to their plight. It was initially created as a temporary organization with the sole responsibility of addressing the needs of refugees in Europe who had been displaced by the Second World War. Over time, however, its geographical focus was extended beyond Europe, and it has subsequently become a prominent international organization with a global focus. Today, UNHCR is widely recognized as the UN's refugee agency and embodies a powerful official in the High Commissioner and a bureaucracy with some 6,500 staff worldwide.

UNHCR's 1950 Statute set out a clear mandate, defining the scope and role of the organization. The Statute defines UNHCR's core mandate as focusing on two principal areas. First, the Office was conceived to work with states to ensure refugees' access to protection. In other words, those outside of their country of origin and with a well-founded fear of persecution would be assured of certain clearly defined rights. Second, it was mandated to ensure that refugees would have access to durable solutions and would either be reintegrated within their country of origin or permanently integrated within a new country. In addition to defining UNHCR's core mandate, the Statute left open the possibility that the scope of the Office's work might be extended at the request of the General Assembly.

Alongside this core mandate, UNHCR is also the guardian of the wider global refugee regime, the main parts of which were created during the same period as the Office. Regimes comprise the norms, rules, principles, and decision-making procedures that regulate the behavior of states. They are generally created by states in order to facilitate international cooperation in a particular issue area, such as trade or the environment. The global refugee regime now includes a number of interstate agreements and practices, which define states' obligations towards refugees. The centerpiece of the regime is the 1951 Convention relating to the Status of Refugees (1951 Convention), which provides a definition of who qualifies for refugee status and sets out the rights to which all refugees are entitled. The Convention also explicitly identifies UNHCR as having supervisory responsibility for its implementation.

In attempting to fulfill its mandate, UNHCR's work has been at the heart of world politics for more than 50 years. States created UNHCR not only for altruistic reasons, but also to promote regional and international stability. Moreover, states sought to create a regime to support functions which serve their interests, such as sharing the costs of granting asylum and coordinating policies regarding the treatment of refugees. UNHCR has consequently been in an ambiguous position of, on the one hand, representing states' interests and being dependent upon donor state funding, and, on the other hand, needing to influence states in order to persuade them to fulfill their humanitarian obligations towards refugees. Finding a balance between these two positions has been a significant and recurring challenge for UNHCR.

UNHCR's task of persuading states to cooperate in the pursuit of refugee protection and durable solutions has been further complicated by the fact that governments' reactions to refugees have often been hostile. Over time, states have become increasingly concerned about movements of people within and across national borders. States in both the global North and South have increasingly come to see the mass arrival and prolonged presence of refugees as a security concern and a burden. Refugees have been identified as a spill-over of conflict, at both a regional and global scale. Refugees have also been perceived as a burden on local and national economies, and have been blamed for increased pressures on social cohesion and national identity. In light of these concerns, UNHCR faces the fundamental challenge of persuading states to meet their obligations towards refugees in spite of their reluctance to provide asylum or to share the burden of refugee protection in other ways.

It is also significant that UNHCR and the global refugee regime were established in the immediate aftermath of the Second World War, which was a time when principles of human rights and justice played a significant role in the establishment and shaping of global institutions. The Cold War, post-Cold War and post-9/11 eras, however, have witnessed rapidly changing political circumstances and changing dynamics of forced displacement. Within this context, the Office has faced the challenge of upholding the regime and ensuring its own institutional survival, while adapting its work to meet the opportunities and constraints posed by the changing context of world politics. In response, UNHCR's core mandate has undergone a number of changes, and the scope of its work has been expanded over time under the authority of the General Assembly. In the 1960s and 1970s, for example, UNHCR became increasingly involved in refugee situations in the Third World. The 1980s saw it take on a growing role in providing assistance in refugee camps and shifting away from its traditional focus on legal protection. The 1990s saw it assume a wider role in providing humanitarian relief and engaging in repatriation operations. The late 1990s and early twenty-first century have seen UNHCR take on ever greater responsibility for the protection of internally displaced persons (IDPs), who, unlike refugees, have not crossed an international border. The expansion of the Office's work to include these new areas has often been controversial, and there have been concerns that UNHCR has been used by states in ways that may contradict or undermine its refugee protection mandate.

In this process of adaptation and expansion, UNHCR has had little material power of its own and has faced the constraints of being dependent upon the voluntary contributions of key donor states and reliant upon host governments for permission to initiate operations on their territory. The organization has not, however, simply been a mechanism through which states act. While UNHCR is constrained by states, the history of the organization makes clear that it is far from a passive mechanism with no independent agenda.[1] Rather, it has, at times, influenced the international political agenda and international responses to humanitarian crises through other sorts of power, such as moral authority and expertise.

In seeking to exert influence in the international system, UNHCR has had to confront a number of significant and recurring challenges.

Paramount among these has been the need to reconsider and adapt the Office's mandate, organization and approach in response to the changing nature of forced displacement over the past half century. In response to the changing interests and priorities of states, UNHCR has also faced the task of facilitating international cooperation to ensure the protection of refugees and to find solutions to their plight. While the challenge of refugees is global, some regions of the world are more affected than others. In fact, the great majority of the world's refugees are now located in global South compared to the less than 5 percent who seek asylum in the North. This concentration of refugees in some of the world's poorest countries has made international cooperation more difficult. At the same time, UNHCR's ability to fulfill its mandate has repeatedly relied upon being able to establish partnerships with other actors within and beyond the UN system. UNHCR, like many other organizations, has therefore repeatedly faced the challenge of how to improve its relationship and collaborate with a wide array of actors. One of the main objectives of this book is to examine how UNHCR has addressed these challenges over time.

An examination of UNHCR's history and evolution also contributes to our understanding of global governance and the role of international organizations. Like many international organizations, UNHCR has been vested with responsibility for upholding a regime. Yet, it has had little power other than moral authority and persuasion to fulfill this task. It has faced the challenge of working within a political environment where power and interests dominate and define outcomes. The Office has therefore faced the question of how to reconcile its normative agenda with the *realpolitik* of changing circumstances. At each stage of its history, this has led to the strategic dilemma of whether and how to adapt its own work and mandate to better serve the interests of states. On the one hand, ignoring the interests of states runs the risk of UNHCR becoming sidelined or irrelevant. On the other hand, adapting its mandate in accordance with the short-term interests of states has risked undermining its moral authority and the humanitarian principles upon which this moral authority is based.

Given the significance of this tension, this book explores how UNHCR has been situated between the constraints and challenges of states' power and interests and its own normative agenda of promoting refugee protection and access to solutions. It explains how UNHCR has attempted to reconcile these competing claims, how it has institutionally adapted over time in order to be better at doing so, and how it might adapt in the future to meet new and emerging

1 The origins of international concern for refugees

While the presence of refugees is one of the hallmarks of contemporary society, refugee flows date back to pre-modern times. In fact, human history is replete with stories of forced migration and exodus, and the importance of sanctuary and the obligation to protect the persecuted are part of all great religious traditions and texts. Throughout early history across Europe and the Middle East, sites of worship were recognized as places of sanctuary and protection, offering refuge to people fleeing wars, political upheavals, and religious strife in near and distant lands.

Refugees only became a significant international issue, however, after the formation of the modern state system in the seventeenth century. With the emergence of centralized states in Europe, local monarchs tried to impose territorial unity on their states and targeted religious minorities and others whose practices deviated from the national norm. In this context, refugees became a more prominent matter of inter-state concern. The Peace of Westphalia of 1648, for example, identified refugees as people who had lost the protection of their own state and recognized the importance of offering asylum to at least some of the world's refugees.[1] For the first time, European sovereigns affirmed a basic right to emigration for those wishing to leave their home countries because their religion differed from that of their monarch.

During this time, however, grants of asylum to refugees were largely *ad hoc* and based on feelings of some kind of religious or political affinity for those seeking refuge. For example, Protestants expelled from France (the Huguenots) following the revocation of the Edict of Nantes in 1685 were accepted as religious confreres by Protestant Britain and a number of other neighboring European states. The Huguenots, however, were also attractive migrants as they brought with them considerable financial assets and commercial, industrial and challenges in world politics. It attempts to critically assess and learn from both the positive and negative consequences of past change and adaptation, and to engage in new thinking about how UNHCR might better adapt to address the ongoing tension between *realpolitik* and upholding refugees' rights.

The book is divided into six chapters. Chapter 1 offers an overview of the emergence of the refugee issue and the context within which UNHCR was created. Chapter 2 examines the historical evolution of the Office during the Cold War, showing how it expanded and evolved to meet the political changes that took place during that era. Chapter 3 explores the Office's relationship to changing world politics in the post-Cold War era. In particular, it focuses on the key changes and initiatives of the Office that have taken place as it tries to respond to new challenges posed by globalization, the post-9/11 era, and the changing nature of conflict. Chapter 4 examines UNHCR as a global institution. It outlines the present-day structure of the Office, its wider relationships to the UN system, and the political challenges that emerge from its structural position. Chapter 5 looks at the changing nature of refugee protection and durable solutions. It assesses how the Office is responding to challenges such as protracted refugee situations and internal displacement, and what these responses mean for the future work of the Office. Finally, the Conclusion offers a forward-looking vision of how UNHCR can respond to its current and future tasks and reflects upon the insights that emerge from focusing on UNHCR and the refugee regime for understanding global governance and the role of institutions in world politics.

military expertise that could be put to good use in their new countries. Shortly after the Huguenot immigration, far less endowed Protestants from Germany (the Palatines) were viewed with hostility and soon rejected. Thus, not all refugees were offered a warm welcome during this era.

Forced migration occurred more frequently during the period of European state consolidation in the nineteenth century, and Britain and the United States, in particular, responded by offering asylum for those fleeing persecution and repression. Following the French Revolution and the 1848 Revolutions in Europe, for example, Britain offered a haven for thousands of émigrés. Throughout this period, the United States also had an open immigration policy and acted as the safety valve for many of Europe's refugees and migrants. As the number of refugees rose, refugees became the subject of increased bilateral negotiations between states by the beginning of the twentieth century, and some elements of modern refugee law began to be formulated in response. Much of this activity, however, remained *ad hoc* and there was no international mechanism for assistance for refugees.

While refugees have been present throughout history, a global refugee regime, comprising a formal international organization for refugees, legal conventions, and an international structure to care for the displaced only began to emerge in the aftermath of the First World War. The creation of a regime regulating states' responses to refugees became increasingly necessary as states began to introduce immigration laws on the basis of race, national passports and other legal and administrative barriers to entry in the late nineteenth and early twentieth centuries, largely in response to the rise of nationalism and the assertion of national sovereignty over their borders. Individuals forced to flee their homelands were subsequently unable to obtain citizenship or legal residence in another country without the required legal documentation, and were therefore in need of international protection. In order to meet this challenge, states began to create an institutional framework that would facilitate multilateral cooperation to meet the needs of the displaced. This chapter therefore explains how the wider political context of the two world wars and the emergence of the Cold War shaped the early global refugee regime, which subsequently led to the creation of UNHCR in 1950.

Refugees and the two world wars

State controls on entry greatly exacerbated the massive refugee crises generated by the First World War and the subsequent break-up of

Europe's multinational empires. Millions of people uprooted by the war and rendered stateless by their former empires, without national passports or identification and consequently without the protection of their home state, moved from country to country in search of refuge. In addition, European governments feared huge flows of displaced persons and rushed to erect protective barriers, close borders and expel thousands of individuals across national frontiers. Such government reactions contributed to huge refugee populations at the start of the 1920s, which threatened regional security in Europe and strained the limited resources of private and public international agencies and individual European governments.

To reduce this source of inter-state tension and to fill the gap in protection, Western governments established the first multilateral coordinating mechanism for refugees in 1921.[2] At the urging of non-governmental organizations, led by the Red Cross movement, the League of Nations created the Office of High Commissioner for Refugees and empowered it with specific responsibilities for protecting particular groups of refugees. Initially, the Office had responsibility for refugees fleeing revolution and civil war in Russia, but this responsibility was later extended to Greek, Turkish, Bulgarian, and Armenian refugees. In the 1930s, the major European governments reached international agreements to protect refugees fleeing from the disintegrating Russian and Ottoman Empires. In later years, these governments extended the agreements to include those fleeing Germany and Austria. Such cooperative achievements were largely the individual work of the first High Commissioner for Refugees, Fridtjof Nansen, who proved to be a highly innovative and successful advocate for refugees. In particular, Nansen developed mechanisms to ensure the legal protection of refugees, internationally recognized documentation to facilitate their travel (the "Nansen Passport"), and cooperated with other international agencies to find solutions for refugees.

Although under the aegis of the League of Nations, the international response to refugees prior to the Second World War did not constitute an effective or an enduring regime. Fearing pressure from a super-governmental authority to recognize political dissidents of any state, governments refrained from adopting a universal definition of "refugee." Instead, Western governments designated only specific national groups as refugees, providing them with only minimal legal rights, and limited the efforts of the High Commissioner by keeping his mandate deliberately narrow and providing him with only a meager budget. As the overall political effectiveness and credibility of the League of Nations declined, particularly after the withdrawal of

Germany, Japan, and Italy from its membership, and after its failure to solve the Manchurian and Ethiopian conflicts during the 1930s, its competence to deal with refugee problems also decreased.

The crucial impediments to genuine international cooperation regarding refugees, however, were the lack of any consistent or coherent international commitment to resolving refugee problems and the existence of an anti-immigration bias in most countries. During the years of the Great Depression in the late 1920s and 1930s, almost every Western nation believed that tight fiscal constraints and high unemployment levels at home should limit any humanitarian initiatives on behalf of refugees from abroad. They also believed that no particular foreign policy benefits would accrue from either putting political and moral pressure on refugee-generating countries or from accepting their unwanted dissidents and minority groups. Thus, despite pleas from public and private refugee organizations for additional resettlement locations for the world's persecuted following the First World War, governments responded with more restrictive responses to the needs of refugees. Most significantly, early efforts at establishing a refugee regime proved to be totally ineffective in responding to refugee and human rights crises facing the international community in the inter-war years, especially the persecution of European Jews. Despite these failures, however, initial international cooperative efforts on behalf of refugees and the establishment of the world's first international refugee agencies provided an important foundation for the global refugee regime, which was established in the aftermath of the Second World War.

The Second World War displaced tens of millions of people, both in Europe and elsewhere. At first, international efforts to solve the post-war refugee problem followed the pattern set in the inter-war period, that is, to set up temporary measures to resolve an emergency situation. The Supreme Headquarters Allied Expeditionary Force (SHAEF) perceived the displaced as a problem of huge proportion and a risk to the social and political order in Europe. SHAEF consequently focused its efforts on coordinating the return to Eastern Europe and the Soviet Union of hundreds of thousands of refugees and displaced persons. However, SHAEF soon ran into controversy when it ignored the wishes of many people who did not wish to return home because they feared persecution at the hands of Communist authorities. In late 1943, the Allied Powers established an intergovernmental body, the United Nations Relief and Rehabilitation Agency (UNRRA), whose principal function was to take over from SHAEF and to oversee the repatriation of the millions of displaced people under Allied control.

But UNRRA was in no sense a refugee organization. Although it was authorized to give temporary relief to those under its care, it was not empowered to arrange for the resettlement of refugees and displaced persons to third countries. Moreover, in accordance with the terms of the February 1945 Yalta Agreements and in response to Soviet pressure, UNRRA played an active part in the controversial forcible repatriation of large numbers of people in Europe.

Several dramatic suicides in the displaced persons camps and bloody confrontations between Western military officials and refugees resisting forced repatriation finally convinced the US military command that the fears of future persecution at the hands of their countries' Communist authorities of many of those remaining in their custody were genuine. As Western powers became increasingly reluctant to return displaced persons to areas under Communist control, the mass repatriations slowed and finally came to halt at the end of 1946.

Overshadowed by the emerging East–West conflict, the issue of repatriation became one of the most contentious issues debated within the early sessions of the newly-formed United Nations. Repatriation touched on the fundamental ideological conflicts dividing East and West. The core of the conflict concerned the rights of people to choose where they wanted to live, to flee from oppression, and to express their own opinions. The West and the Soviet-dominated bloc differed fundamentally on these issues. The Communist countries were concerned that if the refugees remained in the West, they would embarrass and discredit their newly-established regimes. They therefore rejected outright the idea that their citizens could have any valid reason for opposing return and maintained that those who resisted repatriation were war criminals or traitors. The West insisted that displaced persons should have the freedom to choose whether to return home or not. Repatriation as a possible solution to refugee problems consequently became entirely discredited in eyes of Western governments.

The origins of UNHCR, the 1951 Convention and the international refugee regime

The contemporary international approach to refugee problems only emerged fully after UNRRA was abolished in 1947 and was replaced by the International Refugee Organization (IRO). The United States, which provided over 70 percent of UNRAA funds and whose nationals occupied most senior management positions, was deeply critical of its repatriation policies and decided to terminate the organization. In its place, and in the face of adamant opposition from the Soviet Union, the United States worked to create the IRO which focused on resettling the remaining refugees and displaced persons created by the war and its aftermath. With the establishment of the IRO, states recognized the right of refugees not to be repatriated against their will. The international community also adopted, for the first time, a universal definition of refugee based on individualized "persecution or fear of persecution" on the grounds of race, religion, nationality, or political opinion. In so doing, Western powers made refugee eligibility dependent upon the circumstances of the individual rather than membership in a group, and accepted the individual's right to flee from political persecution.

This change constituted a fundamental shift in the approach of international refugee protection. Previously, international organizations had dealt only with specific groups of refugees, and refugee status was therefore dependent on belonging to that group, rather than the specific experience of an individual. In fact, the international community had never attempted to formulate a definition of the term "refugee" and had not tied the concept of refugee to fear of persecution. The experience of persecution during the Second World War and the emergence of human rights and justice as central themes of post-war institutions, however, had a significant impact on the response of states to victims of persecution. Reflecting the spirit of the age, Article 14 of the 1948 Universal Declaration of Human Rights provided that "everyone has the right to seek and enjoy in other countries asylum from persecution." While this so-called right to asylum was not enshrined in future agreements, the shift from group to individual protection and the new emphasis on human rights proved significant for the future direction of international refugee protection.

Western powers hoped that the IRO would achieve two goals: First, to resolve longstanding refugee situations with the potential to destabilize European economies still recovering from the ruins of war, and second, to "internationalize" the refugee problem by distributing refugees and refugee costs among a number of North and South American, Western European, Australasian and African countries. IRO also served the interests of occupied Germany and Western European countries who were concerned about the economic costs of hosting refugee populations. As the principal architect of the post-war refugee regime, the United States not only underwrote over two-thirds of the organization's costs, but also used the IRO to its advantage by maintaining almost exclusive control over the organization's leadership.

In the first year of its existence, the IRO resettled the majority of the refugee caseload it had inherited from UNRRA. It was able to accomplish this because many nations saw recruiting from the displaced persons camps in Europe as one way of addressing their domestic labor shortages following the Second World War and the subsequent period of economic growth. Despite the resettlement achievements of the IRO, however, there remained several hundred thousand displaced persons in camps across Europe at the end of the 1940s who failed to meet the selective admissions policies of several of the resettlement countries. Moreover, with the onset of the Cold War in Europe, refugee problems showed few signs of disappearing as new groups of refugees from Eastern Europe began to make their way westward. At the same time, cataclysmic events in India, Korea, China, and Palestine during the late 1940s and early 1950s, as well as along the perimeter of the Iron Curtain, had all created new refugees by the millions. Given the resulting rise in global refugee numbers, the widespread perception that there were limits to the numbers of refugees resettlement countries would accept, and the belief that the IRO had been an extremely expensive operation, Western officials came to the position that there was an urgent need for a new UN refugee agency.

Despite the scale of the global refugee crisis, however, the US was unwilling to pledge unlimited support to refugees and actively opposed the international community committing itself to unspecified and future responsibilities. Instead, the US had turned decisively to the direct economic assistance of the European countries through the Marshall Plan, a strategy that Washington believed would make it easier for European governments to absorb refugees. This policy shift assumed that the need for exceptional or urgent relief and resettlement measures for European refugees had passed and that the problems that remained were temporary and could be dealt with by a small successor agency to the IRO. From 1943 to 1950, the US had been the leading financial and political supporter of international cooperation on refugees. By 1950, however, US refugee policy was reoriented towards exposing the inadequacies of the Soviet Union and its allies, and to exploit unrest behind the Iron Curtain. With accentuation of these Cold War themes, American perceptions of international organizations dedicated to resolving refugee problems underwent a fundamental shift. International refugee relief operations were curtailed, unilateral initiatives were encouraged, and international organizations unwilling to subordinate themselves to US foreign policy objectives were denied American aid.

Against this background, discussions took place within the United Nations from 1948 to 1950 regarding the termination of the IRO and the creation of a new international refugee organization—UNHCR.[3] While states recognized the need for a specialized international organization to protect refugees, governments differed on what they believed UNHCR's scope and functions should be. The United States sought a temporary refugee agency with narrow authority and limited functions. In particular, the United States sought to deny UNHCR a relief role by depriving it of the authority and the funding to carry out relief assistance operations for refugees. American officials believed that the sole function of the proposed office should be international legal protection. In contrast, the principal Western European governments, such as France and the Benelux countries, were anxious to secure large-scale operational funds for the refugees they were assisting on their territories. Other states who were largely protected from large influxes of refugees by geographic factors, such as the UK, felt that refugees should be the responsibility of host states. Finally, India and Pakistan, who were in the throes of one of the largest population exchanges of modern times following partition in 1947, argued that UNHCR should be a strong permanent organization with global responsibilities and the ability to raise funds for relief assistance.

These competing interests played a central role in determining the functions of UNHCR, the definition of "refugee" it could employ, the autonomy of the Office, the scope of its activities, and the extent to which it would be financially supported as it carried out its work. The resulting Statute of the Office of the High Commissioner for Refugees, adopted by the General Assembly through Resolution 428(V) on 14 December 1950, clearly reflects the interests of the more powerful states in the international system, most notably the United States and the UK. As the details of the Statute make clear, UNHCR was created to serve very specific functions within narrow parameters and with almost no institutional or material autonomy.

As specified by Chapter 1 of the Statute, UNHCR was established to act under the authority of the General Assembly to serve two specific functions: to protect refugees and to find permanent solutions to their plight, either through voluntary repatriation or through their assimilation within new national communities. In this way, the Statute details what continues to be UNHCR's core mandate responsibilities: to provide international protection for refugees and to find durable solutions to their plight, through repatriation, local integration, or the resettlement of refugees to a third country. It is significant that UNHCR's original mandate did not include the provision of material assistance to refugees, a function particularly sought by India and Pakistan, and that the work of the High Commissioner was to be entirely non-political. Also significant was the decision to exclude "internal refugees"—internally displaced people—from UNHCR's mandate.

The Statute further specified the scope of UNHCR's work by defining who qualified as a refugee and by placing a temporal limitation on the High Commissioner's authority. Continuing the trend of defining a refugee in terms of individualized persecution, UNHCR's Statute primarily defined a refugee as any person who was outside their country of origin due to a well-founded fear of persecution due to their race, religion, nationality or political opinion.[4] The Statute also restricted UNHCR's mandate to work only with those individuals who were refugees as a result of events occurring before 1 January 1951, thereby limiting the Office's ability to engage in future refugee emergencies. Finally, UNHCR was only given a limited life by the Statute, which only provided for the existence of the Office until the end of 1953.

Also significant was the limited autonomy given to UNHCR. The Statute specifies that the High Commissioner was to be elected by the General Assembly, was required to follow policy directives issued by the General Assembly, the Economic and Social Council (ECOSOC), or a future advisory committee established by ECOSOC, and report annually to the General Assembly. Perhaps more significant, however, were the limitations placed on the financial autonomy of UNHCR. As specified in paragraph 20 of the Statute, UNHCR was only to receive financial support from the United Nations budget to cover administrative expenditures relating to the functioning of the Office, and that "all other expenditures relating to the activities of the High Commissioner shall be financed by voluntary contributions." In this way, UNHCR was made financially dependent on donor governments. More than 50 years later, this dependence continues to be the most significant means through which states are able to control the scope of UNHCR's work.

As illustrated in the functions, scope, and autonomy given to UNHCR, the Office's establishment in 1950 reflected the political and strategic interests of the major Western powers and, specifically, the United States. By placing severe limitations on UNHCR's functional scope and authority, the United States and its allies sustained their desire to create an international refugee agency that would neither pose a threat to their national sovereignty nor impose new financial obligations on them. In addition, the adoption of persecution as the main characteristic of the Statute's refugee definition was made to fit a Western interpretation of asylum-seekers prevalent in the early Cold War period. The definition had the added advantage of serving ideological purposes by stigmatizing the fledgling Communist regimes as persecutors. It was also perceived to be an appropriate way of dealing with the concerns of religious and ethnic minorities in Europe—especially the Jews—who were anxious to ensure that in the event of future persecutions, international arrangements existed for facilitating departure and resettlement elsewhere.

Negotiations to establish UNHCR coincided with the drafting of a UN refugee convention, intended not only to enshrine the universal refugee definition, but to more clearly define the rights of those individuals recognized as refugees. Only 26 countries participated in the subsequent negotiations, and none, except Yugoslavia, were from the Soviet bloc. During these negotiations, Western governments, led by the United States and France, argued for limiting the responsibilities of states who were signatories to the convention. The British argued for a broad global definition covering all refugees, wherever located, who were then seeking asylum and others who might require asylum in the future. The United States and France considered that if governments were expected to adhere to the convention they should know in advance precisely for which refugees, in what numbers, and in what places they were to undertake commitments.

In the end, the view that the refugee convention should serve mainly as an instrument for the legal protection of European refugees prevailed. Thus, whereas UNHCR's Statute placed no geographical limits on the High Commissioner's mandate, the 1951 Convention relating to the Status of Refugees defined the obligations of signatory nations more narrowly. Like the Statute, the 1951 Convention covered only those who were refugees as a result of "events occurring before 1 January 1951," but governments were given the additional discretion to apply it only to those who were refugees "owing to events in Europe" or "owing to events in Europe and elsewhere."

The 1951 Convention also defined a list of rights for refugees. Because refugees are individuals who have fled their home country and no longer enjoy the legal protections afforded to citizens of a state, the framers of the Convention stipulated that refugees should have access to national courts, the right to employment and education, and a host of other social, economic and civil rights on a par with nationals of the host country. However, states decided not to grant refugees a right to asylum, notwithstanding the provisions of the 1948 Universal Declaration of Human Rights.

Perhaps the most significant right granted to refugees by the 1951 Convention is *non-refoulement*: the right of refugees not to be returned to a country where they risk persecution. *Non-refoulement* remains the cornerstone of international refugee protection, and is now considered to be a provision of customary international law, binding even on states not party to the 1951 Convention.[5] It would also become central to the later principle of voluntary repatriation, as states were prohibited from repatriating refugees until the dangers that confronted them in their home country had disappeared. Moreover, refugees themselves had the choice of deciding either to voluntarily return to their home countries or remain in exile.[6]

In addition to these strict parameters on the scope of its activities, it is important to note that UNHCR came into existence at the start of the Cold War and at a time of growing tensions between East and West. Refugee protection became further embedded in world politics as the Cold War progressed, and UNHCR would face extraordinary pressures and obstacles in providing protection to refugees and in devising solutions to their problems. The nascent Office would only be able to surmount these challenges by reframing refugee protection as a Cold War issue and by expanding its focus away from a Eurocentric basis to a global one. Such a response would have a dramatic effect not only on the work of UNHCR in the following decades, but also on its relationship with states and their interpretation of the Office's mandate.

2 UNHCR in the Cold War, 1950–1991

No international organization has had such an unpromising beginning as UNHCR. The first UN High Commissioner for Refugees, Gerrit Jan van Heuven Goedhart (1951–1956), had a mandate to protect refugees and to provide solutions to refugee problems, but he had only three years to demonstrate the Office's relevance and practically no funds with which to carry out his work. Determined to keep UNHCR a strictly limited agency and to restrict their own obligations to costly refugee resettlement, states provided very little financial support to UNHCR in its early days. The United States did not fund UNHCR until 1955 and chose instead to generously fund rival humanitarian agencies, including its own refugee office, the US Escapee Program, that were closely aligned to American foreign policy interests. From its inception, UNHCR tried to overcome these financial and operational restrictions. The High Commissioner realized that without a bigger budget the Office would have no program worthy of the name, enjoy little, if any, autonomy, and would exercise limited influence in the international system.

Not only did Goedhart have few resources at his disposal but the Office was also confronted with a number of legal limits on its activities. UNHCR's mandate only allowed the Office to offer protection to those who were refugees as "a result of events occurring before 1 January 1951." The Statute also precluded the organization from conferring refugee status on an entire national population fleeing a repressive government but instead could confer such status only on individuals whose claims had to be assessed on a case-by-case basis. People fleeing from international or civil conflicts, economic hardship, famines or natural disasters were excluded from UNHCR's protection. Moreover, the 1951 Convention refugee definition contained both geographical and temporal restrictions. It was intended to be used by the Western states in dealing with arrivals from Eastern Europe, and consequently reflected the international politics of the early Cold War period.

Perhaps most significantly, the scope and extent of the authority of the High Commissioner were further limited by the importance attached by states to the international norms of sovereignty and non-intervention in the domestic affairs of states. UNHCR's Statute restricted the authority of the High Commissioner to assist refugees who had crossed international borders and expressly forbade the High Commissioner from involving himself in political activities.[1] Because the causes of refugee flows were considered to fall outside the organization's humanitarian and "non-political" mandate set out in its Statute, UNHCR was reluctant to become involved in human rights monitoring. UNHCR officials were also inclined to avoid raising delicate political questions when dealing with host governments for fear of overstepping their mandate or damaging relations with governments, most of whom would consider such intrusions to be interference in their internal affairs. During most of the Cold War, the norms of sovereignty and non-intervention limited the scope of UNHCR activity and, with few exceptions, restricted the Office to work in countries of asylum rather than countries of origin.

Throughout the Cold War, UNHCR approached the refugee problem in a manner which can be characterized as reactive, exile-oriented and refugee-centric.[2] The Office primarily worked with people after they had fled across borders to neighboring countries where they required protection and assistance. UNHCR staff concentrated their activities on assisting refugees in camps or settlements and negotiating with host and donor governments for support, and paid little attention to preventing or averting refugee movements. It placed primary responsibility for solving refugee problems on states that hosted refugees rather than on states that caused refugees to flee. Hence, UNHCR emphasized local settlement and resettlement rather than repatriation as solutions for refugee problems.

In the initial years of its existence, UNHCR faced seemingly insuperable obstacles to fulfilling its mandate. The framers of UNHCR, particularly the United States, did not want the Office to assume the role and responsibility of an international relief agency and deliberately limited UNHCR to the sole function of international legal protection.[3] UNHCR was not allowed to administer any programs of material assistance despite the existence of an estimated 400,000 destitute displaced persons in Europe who had been passed over for overseas resettlement during the IRO period and who were now the High Commissioner's direct responsibility. UNHCR was restricted to concerning itself with international legal protection for these refugees, without actually contributing anything of a concrete nature to finding a solution to their plight. In his early speeches before the UN, Goedhart bristled at these restrictions and hammered home the view that there was an urgent need to integrate the hundreds of thousands of unwanted displaced people who were "warehoused" in camps throughout Europe many years after the end of the war. The High Commissioner observed that, if these conditions persisted, the problems of refugees would fester and there was a real danger that his Office would simply "administer misery."

The fledgling UNHCR was, therefore, faced with the challenge of expanding its mandate and finding innovative ways to protect, assist and find solutions not only for the displaced people left over from the Second World War but also for the millions of people who would become refugees around the world in future years. Although UNHCR was created with very little independence and could only act under the strict guidelines outlined in its Statute, it soon became apparent that the High Commissioner could exploit his authority in order to expand his Office's functions and operations in ways compatible with refugee needs. UNHCR enjoyed considerable moral authority based on its role as protector and diffuser of international refugee law and standards. Successive High Commissioners portrayed UNHCR as an apolitical and impartial humanitarian organization which gave the Office considerable leverage in its negotiations with governments. States perceived UNHCR as possessing unique expertise and experience on refugee law and refugee movements and came to depend on the organization for advice and information. As a result, UNHCR eventually acquired considerable independence as it simultaneously tried to define the refugee issue for states, to convince governments that refugee problems were solvable, to prescribe solutions, and to monitor their implementation. In the process, UNHCR would undergo a remarkable transition during the next three decades from being a marginal international agency encumbered with numerous restrictions to a global organization with growing autonomy and authority to shape the behavior of states as well as provide protection and assistance to the world's displaced. In order to highlight this transition, this chapter examines the emergence and adaptation of UNHCR during the Cold War era. In particular, it considers UNHCR's initial role in post-war Europe and its struggle for legitimacy; the reasons for the Office's gradual expansion beyond Europe from the late 1950s; and the ways in which successive High Commissioners since the 1960s have responded to the challenges of displacement at the different key political junctures of the Cold War.

UNHCR and the Cold War in Europe

When UNHCR was established in December 1950, Europe was the principal area of US and international refugee concern as the Cold War intensified and new refugee flows moved from East to West. The Eurocentric orientation of UNHCR reflected not only the international political environment but also the foreign policy priorities of the United States and the other major Western governments. Most importantly, the American preoccupation with reconstruction and rehabilitation efforts in Europe after the Second World War and the rapidly developing Cold War critically affected the lens through which Washington viewed both its own refugee policy and UNHCR.[4] US policy-makers soon considered refugee issues within the same policy framework as national security. US generosity towards refugees from Eastern Europe was in part motivated by a desire to "roll back", or at least contain, Communism by encouraging East European citizens to escape their homelands. Refugees also became important symbols in the ideological rivalry of the early Cold War. "Escapees" who crossed over to the West "voted with their feet" and represented a significant political and ideological asset for the West.

In the early 1950s, American leaders considered refugee policy as too important to US national security interests to permit the United Nations overall control. To US policy-makers, the most important aspects of American refugee policy were maintaining international attention devoted to refugees from Communist countries, encouraging emigration from the Eastern bloc, and minimizing international appeals for assistance funds to refugees.[5] Throughout the early years of UNHCR's existence, the United States consequently sought to severely limit the Office's functional scope and independence and to marginalize its influence. Washington created several American-led refugee organizations which were generously funded and supported US foreign policy objectives. Thus, UNHCR was confronted from the beginning by rival agencies and non-governmental organizations (NGOs) who encroached on its modest jurisdiction and received the great bulk of American and other funding. The denial of American financial and diplomatic support directly affected the organization's ability to define an independent role for itself in its first five years of its existence.[6]

Despite the opposition of the United States, UNHCR soon began to exercise power autonomously in ways unintended by states. High Commissioner Goedhart enlarged the scope of his Office by obtaining the capacity to independently raise funds and by assuming material assistance responsibilities. With a grant from the Ford Foundation in

1952, UNHCR involved itself for the first time in providing assistance to NGOs to promote the integration of refugees in Western European asylum countries. This funding also enabled UNHCR to take the lead role in responding to a refugee crisis in West Berlin in early 1953, thereby demonstrating its usefulness to the major powers, raising the Office's international profile and laying the groundwork for an eventual softening of the US position regarding UNHCR. These early successes legitimized the need for UNHCR material assistance to Europe's protracted refugee populations and directly led to the establishment of a UNHCR program for permanent solutions and emergency assistance.

The world's first major Cold War refugee crisis was the Hungarian crisis of November 1956. The invasion of Hungary by the Soviet Army precipitated the mass exodus of nearly 200,000 refugees to neighboring Austria and Yugoslavia. Overwhelmed by the influx of refugees, Austria formally requested UNHCR to appeal to governments on its behalf for assistance in responding to the emergency. UNHCR immediately established a coordinating group, comprising a number of leading inter-governmental organizations and NGOs. In both Austria and Yugoslavia, the High Commissioner's local representatives chaired the groups that administered the emergency aid, thereby demonstrating that it was the only agency capable of coordinating both international refugee relief and the collection of funds for emergency material assistance. This paved the way for the General Assembly to designate UNHCR as the "lead agency" to direct the international emergency operation for Hungarian refugees in 1956.

To extend aid to fleeing Hungarians, the organization had to overcome some of the legal restrictions imposed on its activities by its Statute. To overcome the temporal limitations embedded in the refugee definition, the new High Commissioner, Auguste Lindt (1956–1960), argued that the causes of the flight of Hungarians could be traced to events before 1951 and therefore action was within UNHCR's mandate. The other legal hurdle to be overcome was that UNHCR was supposed to determine on a case-by-case basis the status of each refugee. Lindt argued that this was impossible in an emergency situation. UNHCR, therefore, made no attempt to judge individual motives for flight but approved all Hungarians in Austria and Yugoslavia as *prima facie* refugees, deferring the individual refugee determination process until a later stage.

Through its involvement, UNHCR was able to ensure a successful resolution of the Hungarian refugee crisis by raising the required funds to assist countries of first asylum and by finding solutions for refugees, either through resettlement to a third country or through repatriation to Hungary. UNHCR's successful role in the Hungarian operation demonstrated to states the importance of having an international agency to deal with the humanitarian consequences of international and regional conflict. It also underscored the necessity of finding ways to overcome the restrictive features of the refugee definition contained in UNHCR's Statute and the 1951 Convention if the problems of addressing mass refugee flows were to be addressed adequately. As a consequence of its work for Hungarian refugees, UNHCR also won the confidence of the United States, who would subsequently become its principal donor state. The funding capacities and operational services of UNHCR consequently expanded significantly. Thus, largely on its own initiatives, UNHCR grew from a strictly non-operational agency with no authority to appeal for funds to an institution with a long-range program emphasizing not only protection but increasingly material assistance.

UNHCR expansion into the developing world: the "good offices" approach

Even while UNHCR was preoccupied with refugee problems in Europe, the Office was taking initial steps to lay the groundwork for an expansion of its activities to the developing world. Since the end of the Second World War, demands for independence from European colonies in Africa and Asia had increased dramatically. The process of decolonization not only resulted in a dramatic increase in membership in the UN, but also had significant implications for the work of UNHCR. In French-controlled Algeria and in the Portuguese colonies of Angola, Guinea-Bissau, and Mozambique, the decolonization process was violent and involved massive displacements of refugees. In addition, the British colony of Hong Kong attracted massive numbers of refugees from the Communist regime in China.

UNHCR began to face pressure from newly-independent UN member states to provide these new refugees with international assistance. However, the Office faced acute political problems arising from these new groups. Unlike in Europe, where refugee problems were perceived in an exclusively East–West context, refugee situations in the developing world were considerably different. In many cases, refugee situations directly involved either the political interests of the Western colonial powers, who were also among the founding members of UNHCR, or the security concerns of the newly independent states, who were the newest members of the United Nations. In such cases,

UNHCR sought to avoid the embarrassment of treating refugees fleeing the colonies and territories of their supporters and close allies as victims of persecution. As a consequence, a distinctly new way to respond to refugee problems emerged within the United Nations. Whenever refugee situations appeared with political dynamics and problems that did not correspond with those of the European situation, which were not covered in UNHCR's Statute, or which involved one or more of the Western powers, the General Assembly, increasingly dominated by post-colonial states, granted the High Commissioner new authority so that he could take action. Thus, for the next several decades, states were willing to turn to UNHCR whenever its services could be usefully applied to meet the needs of new and different groups of refugees and displaced persons.

This new approach was termed the "good offices" formula which involved the General Assembly granting UNHCR the authority to raise funds or to initiate assistance programs for operations outside its usual mandate. It was applied in the first instance to raise funds for Chinese refugees in Hong Kong in the mid-1950s. Some 700,000 Chinese refugees had flooded into the British colony of Hong Kong in the two years after the establishment of the People's Republic of China and were in desperate need of assistance. There were, however, formidable political and legal problems regarding the refugee eligibility of the Chinese newcomers in Hong Kong that had to be overcome before UNHCR could become involved. In particular, it was unclear whether the Chinese refugees in Hong Kong fell within UNHCR's mandate. These problems were finally resolved in November 1957 when the General Assembly declared the Chinese refugees "to be of concern to the international community," thereby making it possible for UNHCR to assist refugees who were not normally part of its mandate and without making a determination that the country of refugee origin was persecuting its citizens. Finally, UNHCR was authorized to use its "good offices" to help coordinate and provide much needed material assistance to Chinese refugees in Hong Kong.

Even more significant to UNHCR's expansion into the developing world was the Office's response to the Algerian refugee crisis.[7] In May 1957, Tunisia requested material assistance from UNHCR for the 85,000 Algerian refugees who had fled across the border during the previous two and a half years. This was the first occasion in which UNHCR emergency assistance had been requested in the Third World, and consequently marked an important step in the development both of the political conditions under which the organization had to act and of the functions it was permitted to perform.

The decision to offer assistance to Algerian refugees engendered intense debate within UNHCR about its future role in the developing world.[8] Some within the organization believed that UNHCR should remain focused on its specific mandate to find solutions for the thousands of refugees remaining in Europe. In contrast, High Commissioner Lindt felt that the Tunisian request presented an opportunity for UNHCR to use the new international support and goodwill that the Office had earned as a result of its response to the Hungarian refugee emergency to confirm its position as the leading international refugee agency and as the only international organization able to adapt to new emergencies wherever they arose. Moreover, UNHCR's decision to intervene in the Hungarian refugee emergency on the basis that all the Hungarians *prima facie* fell under UNHCR's mandate and that it was impossible in a mass exodus to screen each asylum seeker individually had established a precedent for action which was difficult for UNHCR to ignore in the Algerian case. Lindt feared that UNHCR would be accused of discriminatory treatment if it neglected the Algerians and he did not want to be perceived as the "High Commissioner for European refugees only."[9] He felt that UNHCR's mandate as defined in its Statute was worldwide and that his Office had responsibility for dealing "with completely different people and not only refugees from communism."[10] He was concerned that to refuse assistance to Tunisia would estrange the organization from a growing bloc of developing countries.

The decision to aid Algerian refugees was not easy, however, and UNHCR had to overcome strong opposition from the colonial power, France. The French government denied UNHCR the authority to give assistance in this case, claiming that Algeria was an integral part of the state of France and that the eventual solution could only be the return to Algeria of the people who had taken refuge in Tunisia and Morocco. France also feared UNHCR involvement would internationalize the crisis, and major Western governments were unwilling to oppose the French. Nevertheless, Lindt persisted and French resistance to UNHCR involvement was eventually overcome through a combination of diplomacy and demonstration of moral authority.

Working with the League of Red Cross Societies as its principal operational partner, UNHCR initially launched an emergency relief program and later a return and reintegration program for over 180,000 Algerian refugees. Tripartite arrangements were used to formalize the involvement and responsibilities of host states, the country of origin and UNHCR. The provision of reintegration and reconstruction assistance, not only to returning refugees but to the community at large in countries of origin, was also a model for future repatriations. In this way, UNHCR's approach to the return of Algerians became a blueprint for UNHCR actions and policies in practically all subsequent repatriations during the 1960s and 1970s.

In the view of many developing countries, UNHCR's action on behalf of Algerians also signified a turning point in the Office's geographical scope and function. The Algerian operation was a bridgehead leading to a period of both global and institutional growth for the organization, and these initiatives laid the groundwork for UNHCR expansion into the developing world in the 1960s. In his four short years as High Commissioner, Lindt had overseen a remarkable transition in UNHCR from its being a sideshow to centerstage in world politics. In his final address to his Executive Committee in 1960, Lindt noted that the Office had to remain flexible and elastic in responding to new refugee situations. Little did he realize the momentous challenges that would confront the next High Commissioner, particularly in Africa.

The Cold War, the Third World and UNHCR: 1960s through the 1980s

During the 1960s and 1970s, the Cold War extended beyond Europe into parts of the developing world. Superpower rivalry, violent decolonization, and post-independence conflict in Africa generated vast numbers of refugees and underscored the strategic importance of conflicts outside of Europe.[11] Both the East and the West were vying for influence in Africa and Asia, while simultaneously trying to minimize the possibilities of their ideological and strategic opponents gaining political advantage in these regions. Throughout the Third World, the United States and the Soviet Union competed to build up local allies. Through a combination of economic aid, political support and weapons deliveries, both superpowers constructed a range of client regimes, which included both governments and liberation movements.[12]

As part of the geopolitics of the Cold War, the United States perceived refugee problems in the Third World as possible sources of instability which the Soviet Union could exploit. Western governments consequently came to see assistance to refugees as a central part of their foreign policy towards newly independent states. During this period, governments made little distinction between military aid, development assistance and refugee relief aid. More importantly, because UNHCR was a Western-dominated and donor-dependent organization, there was little risk of multilateral refugee aid being used in ways unacceptable to the principal donor governments. Western governments were therefore willing to politically and financially support UNHCR's operational expansion into the developing world. At the same time, the addition of newly independent African and Asian member states in the United Nations and the addition of a number of newly independent African nations to UNHCR's Executive Committee made it possible to pass successive General Assembly resolutions which authorized UNHCR to assist a broad category of people displaced by conflict outside of Europe. UNHCR consequently re-oriented its funding from Europe to Africa, with one half of the High Commissioner's annual program budget allocated to African and other Third World projects by 1964.

The two High Commissioners during this period, Felix Schnyder (1960–1965) and Sadruddin Aga Khan (1965–1977), were both politically astute and anticipated the major political transformations in the international system, namely decolonization and the emergence of newly independent states in Africa and Asia. Both High Commissioners also foresaw that these changes in the international system would generate massive refugee movements. They also realized that the traditional refugee concepts and legal definitions that the Office had used in Europe would not apply in developing countries and took steps to expand the Office's global reach.

UNHCR under Felix Schnyder

When Felix Schnyder replaced Lindt as High Commissioner in 1960, he predicted a shift in UNHCR away from programs involving European refugees to a focus on assistance to refugees in the developing world. He also foresaw the need to rely on the authority of the "good offices" resolutions to respond to new refugee emergencies and to undertake new tasks.[13] In order to respond quickly and effectively to new refugee situations in the developing world, Schnyder actively sought to shape states' views on the changing global nature of refugee problems. In particular, he sought and gained state approval to remove many of the constraints imposed on UNHCR's future action by its mandate. In response, the General Assembly passed a series of resolutions that provided the Office with the authority to respond to new situations around the world and allow it to provide assistance to displaced people who did not strictly qualify as refugees under UNHCR's Statute.[14] In 1961, the General Assembly gave the High Commissioner the authority to assist both "refugees within his mandate and those for whom he extends his good offices," effectively removing the legal and institutional barriers to future UNHCR action for non-mandate refugees. In 1965, the General Assembly abandoned altogether the distinction between new groups of refugees covered by "good offices" and UNHCR's mandate refugees and requested the High Commissioner to "pursue his efforts with a view to ensuring an adequate international protection of refugees and to providing satisfactory permanent solutions to the problems affecting the various groups of refugees within his competence."

Under Schnyder, UNHCR also progressively increased its range of programs for both refugees and host populations and governments. The Office's expansion in the developing world coincided with the growing post-colonial membership in the United Nations and the increasing recognition of the economic and political problems of the Third World. Trade, development issues and other issues of importance to the developing world began to dominate the UN agenda and new UN bodies reflecting these concerns emerged. UNHCR took advantage of these events to enhance its own institutional growth and to expand its programs, particularly in Africa. Schnyder came to envisage the Office's own work in Africa as part of the total UN effort to assist developing countries with their modernization and development. Recognizing that African refugee situations were but one aspect of the overall economic and social problem of underdevelopment, the High Commissioner believed that for refugee assistance programs to be effective, they had to be part of the larger development program in a host country.[15] UNHCR acknowledged that this broader developmental approach would necessitate an active role for UN agencies and NGOs other than UNHCR. Schnyder consequently began to cooperate with other agencies, such as the International Labour Organization (ILO), the UN Development Program (UNDP) and the Lutheran World Federation (LWF), to establish rural settlement schemes for refugees as well as host communities across Africa.

With UNHCR's new emphasis on assistance to refugees in developing countries, divisions emerged within the organization over the Office's policy priorities. The High Commissioner believed that in situations such as those in Africa, the major and immediate need of refugees was for emergency and development assistance rather than international legal protection. Schnyder and those running UNHCR's Assistance Division argued that the provision of material assistance to refugees would improve the economic position of the displaced and eventually improve their legal position in their new society. However, not everyone in the organization agreed with this position. The Legal

Division argued that legal status for refugees was as important for their integration in host societies as material assistance, and complained that the Office's staff in Africa gave little time to the legal problems of protection in the region. As later sections of this book illustrate, these tensions between protection and assistance within UNHCR would become even more pronounced in later decades.

As new refugee groups emerged in the 1960s, however, it became increasingly apparent that existing international legal norms were not suitable for dealing with refugee issues in the developing world. Refugees in Africa and Asia had not fled as a result of conditions in Europe before 1951 nor could many of them meet the individual persecution criteria outlined in the international legal instruments. While the good offices resolutions passed by the General Assembly made many refugee groups the concern of UNHCR, the measures were only recommendations and did not impose any legal obligations on states. Consequently, Schnyder and UNHCR's Executive Committee set out to delete the geographic and temporal limitations from the 1951 Convention. This was accomplished in 1967, after Schnyder had left his post, when a Protocol Relating to the Status of Refugees was signed by many nations including some states that were not party to the original convention, most notably the United States. An important effect of the 1967 Protocol was that it brought the 1951 Convention into line with the universal mandate of the Statute of UNHCR.

During the mid-1960s, a number of developing countries also expressed dissatisfaction that the international refugee instruments did not reflect the realities of the refugee situation in the Third World. For example, in 1964, the Organization of African Unity (OAU) formed a Commission on Refugee Problems in Africa and, in collaboration with UNHCR, drafted its own regional refugee instrument. The most important feature of the 1969 OAU Refugee Convention was that the OAU extended the definition of refugee to include not only the 1951 Convention definition but also "every person who, owing to external aggression, occupation, foreign domination or events seriously disturbing public order ... is compelled to leave his place of habitual residence."[16] A decade and a half later, the Cartagena Declaration of 1984 also went further than the 1951 Convention by including "persons who had fled their country because their lives, safety or freedom have been threatened by generalized violence, foreign aggression, internal conflicts, massive violations of human rights or other circumstances which have seriously disturbed public order."[17] These regional legal norms were in fact much more inclusive and in keeping with the actual causes of flight in Africa, Central America, and other parts of the world than were the 1951 Convention and the 1967 Protocol. Most significantly, they responded to the fact that many refugees were fleeing generalized violence and severe human rights violations in which it was often impossible for asylum seekers to generate documented evidence of individual persecution as required by the 1951 Convention.

UNHCR under Sadruddin Aga Khan

From its expansion into Africa in the 1960s, UNHCR under Sadruddin Aga Khan rapidly evolved into a truly global organization during the next decade. Refugee emergencies emerged on all continents, multiplied and took on numerical proportions previously unknown to UNHCR. Faced with mass exoduses from East Pakistan, Uganda, and Indochina, with highly politicized refugee crises in Chile and Argentina, and with the repatriation and reintegration of refugees and internally displaced persons in South Sudan, UNHCR embarked on new assistance programs in a number of refugee and "refugee-like" situations around the world. From a small and mostly non-operational agency focused primarily on legal protection and the promotion of international refugee instruments, UNHCR quickly evolved into the world's most important humanitarian organization.

To facilitate this expansion into operations, there occurred further enlargement of refugee law and "good offices" doctrine, making UNHCR the coordinator of international assistance to refugees and victims of "man-made" disasters and opening up limited assistance channels for certain instances of internal displacement.[18] To facilitate the repatriation of Sudanese refugees who had taken refuge in neighboring countries and to help those who had been internally displaced to return to their homes after the 1972 Addis Ababa Agreement, the General Assembly, for the first time, mentioned refugees and internally displaced side by side in a resolution. In 1975 and 1979, the General Assembly requested the High Commissioner to promote lasting and speedy solutions for refugees and displaced persons "wherever they occur." The legal expansion of his authority gave Sadruddin tremendous scope to engage UNHCR in massive material assistance programs throughout the world.

Sadruddin was determined to enhance UNHCR's independence and to make the Office the most important international humanitarian organization. He largely accomplished these objectives. During this period, the UN created the Office of the United Nations Disaster Relief Coordinator (UNDRO), the first of many attempts to integrate the various UN activities involving assistance to countries experiencing natural disasters and humanitarian emergencies. UNHCR fought fiercely to maintain control over its own operations and successfully resisted UNDRO's efforts to subordinate the Office. Similar tensions between UNHCR and other UN agencies would become a familiar feature of the UN landscape in the decades ahead.

By the 1970s, the scale of humanitarian disasters and the numbers of NGOs and specialized agencies within the UN system had grown so significantly that overall coordination of relief work was essential if international humanitarian action was necessary. In the absence of an effective inter-agency mechanism, the UN Secretary-general, Kurt Waldheim, repeatedly called on Sadruddin to coordinate UN humanitarian and relief programs during this time. UNHCR's assumption of the role of "focal point," which was first used in the 1971 East Pakistan/Bangladesh crisis, became an acceptable international arrangement to coordinate the activities of the UN in a major humanitarian emergency when the technical and material needs would exceed the mandate and capacity of any one agency. These would be the first of many refugee crises in which UNHCR would be called upon by the Secretary-General to act as the UN lead agency for the coordination of international humanitarian assistance. In 1976, ECOSOC confirmed UNHCR's new coordinating function as an integral part of its enlarged competence when it requested the High Commissioner "to continue his activities in cooperation with governments, UN bodies, appropriate inter-governmental organizations and voluntary agencies, to alleviate the suffering of all those of concern to his Office." The same resolution identified persons of concern to be "refugee and displaced persons, victims of man-made disasters, requiring urgent humanitarian assistance." In the process, UNHCR developed an enormous agenda, greatly expanded its overall functions and authority, and became an indispensable and autonomous actor in many of the major political developments in Africa, Asia, and Central America.

Another prominent feature of the 1970s was the renewed importance and use of resettlement as a durable solution. Military *coups d'état* and repression in countries such as Argentina, Chile, Greece, the Soviet Union, Uganda, Uruguay, and Vietnam greatly increased global awareness of human rights violations and spurred greater human rights advocacy. International human rights organizations such as Amnesty International were established and a trans-national human rights advocacy network emerged. At the same time, US and European policy-makers became interested in human rights issues and began to pass legislation incorporating human rights considerations into their foreign and security agendas. In this new international political environment, there was strong support for "rescuing" victims of human rights abuses through overseas resettlement programs. The growth of the international human rights movement directly affected most states' willingness to cooperate with UNHCR and to contribute generously to its resettlement programs.

The ever-growing number of refugee situations around the world led to a substantial increase in the staff of UNHCR, its working budget, and above all on the amount spent on assistance and repatriation programs. Annual program expenditure leapt from US$8.3 million in 1970 to US$69 million in 1975. In the early 1970s, UNHCR organized a number of massive repatriation operations in rapid succession, in particular the East Bengalis in 1972 and the Sudanese in 1973. In each of these cases, the General Assembly requested not only the return of refugees but also their "rehabilitation and resettlement." This further expansion of UNHCR functions soon became standard practice. Thus, when the independence of the former Portuguese territories in Africa led to the return of hundreds of thousands of persons to Guinea-Bissau in 1974–1975, and to Mozambique and Angola in 1975–1976, it was accompanied by rehabilitation programs that incorporated longer-term development planning. In addition to its regular activities, UNHCR also coordinated UN-wide humanitarian programs during this time with budgets in the hundreds of millions of dollars. Consequently, UNHCR's budget for special operations grew thirty-fold between 1966 and 1975. By the mid-1970s, UNHCR's transformation from a small legal protection agency to the world's largest humanitarian relief organization was complete.

The 1980s: global challenges to asylum

While the 1960s and 1970s were decades of expansion for UNHCR, the 1980s ushered in a new era of restrictions and challenges. Economic recession and the election of conservative governments in many Western states led to a shift away from the focus on human rights that had defined the post-war era and resulted in the introduction of increasingly restrictive asylum policies which diminished the authority of UNHCR in the global North. At the same time, the rise of super-power rivalry and regional conflicts, especially in Africa, Asia and Central America, resulted in massive refugee movements in the Third World that proved difficult to resolve and contributed to more restrictive asylum policies across much of the global South. While UNHCR was able to help resolve some of the most difficult refugee crises, notably the plight of the Indochinese refugees and refugees in Central America, the end of the Cold War in 1989 left many large and pro-tracted refugee population in Africa and Asia. Three High Commissioners during this period—Poul Hartling (1978–1985), Jean-Pierre Hocké (1986–1989), and Thorvald Stoltenberg (1990)—tried to respond to these challenges in the North and South. Their success, however, was significantly limited by increasingly restrictive asylum policies, a shift in relations between UNHCR and states, and a significant decline in donor support for the work of UNHCR.

During most of the 1960s and 1970s, UNHCR experienced few of the kinds of asylum problems in the industrialized states that would confront the Office in later decades. Most Western governments acknowledged that UNHCR possessed unrivaled specialized knowledge and expertise concerning refugee law and deferred to the Office's authority on asylum policy. With the notable exception of the United States, UNHCR played an active role in the refugee determination procedures of many industrialized states and exerted a considerable influence over government decisions. The Office's claim to neutrality and apolitical decision-making, coupled with its expert status and authority in refugee law, enabled UNHCR to exert great influence in Europe. Not surprisingly, it was during this period that the legal norms and rules became the *raison d'être* of UNHCR. These permeated the culture of the Office and greatly empowered the Division of Legal Protection over other parts of the organization. Hence, UNHCR's autonomy was enhanced and most governments in Western Europe demonstrated a generally liberal attitude towards asylum seekers.

By the mid-1980s, however, vastly larger numbers of people were traveling from the Third World to Western Europe and North America to claim asylum. In previous decades, most refugees appearing in the West had fled well-publicized persecution in Communist countries and were accepted into the West with little scrutiny into their motives for departure. The intensification of the Cold War across the Third World in the 1980s, coupled with the expansion of air travel, allowed tens of thousands of refugees to travel from regions of conflict in developing countries to claim asylum in the West. Particularly disturbing to Western governments was the fact that asylum applicants increasingly bypassed established refugee-processing channels. Unlike the millions who endured the rigors of camp life in the developing world, the new asylum seekers either independently took the initiative to secure safety in the West or turned to immigrant-trafficking organizations to purchase false documents that enabled them to travel to industrialized countries. Western governments regarded such activities as illegal and branded asylum seekers as opportunists, bogus refugees, and queue jumpers.

In the spring of 1980, an asylum crisis of unparalleled dimensions in US history profoundly affected the future direction of American asylum policy. In April, the first wave of boats that would eventually bring 130,000 Cubans to Florida over a five-month period arrived on American shores. By the end of 1980, these Cubans had been joined by over 11,000 Haitian boat people and by an indeterminate number of Iranians, Nicaraguans, and Ethiopians seeking asylum. The US asylum system was completely overwhelmed by the arrival of over 150,000 asylum seekers in 1980. This mass influx of asylum seekers reached crisis proportions at the same time the US government had officially resettled nearly 200,000 refugees from Indo-China (as dis- cussed below). In 1980 alone, 800,000 immigrants and refugees—more than those entering all the other industrialized countries combined— entered the United States legally while hundreds of thousands of Mexicans and others entered illegally.

As the asylum system became hopelessly blocked, the attitude of the American public grew hostile to refugees. The problems of asylum seekers and refugees came to be linked in the public mind with the problem of illegal aliens and thus fanned the public fear of hordes of uncontrolled illegal immigrants crossing US borders almost at will. During the early 1980s, in addition to the waves of Cuban and Hai- tian "boat people," huge numbers of Salvadorans and Guatemalans, fleeing death squads and violent civil conflicts in their home countries, became "feet people," crossed the US border and sought refuge in the United States.

In direct response to these developments, the US government adopted a number of restrictive measures and deterrents, including the interdiction on the high seas by the US Coast Guard of boats carrying refugees, widespread use of detention of asylum seekers, denial of due process, and swift deportation. UNHCR protested regularly during this period about these developments and appealed to the American authorities to honor the commitments for refugee protection that the United States had made in signing the 1967 Protocol. The United States flatly rejected all UNHCR criticisms of its asylum policy and UNHCR was unable to exert significant pressure on Washington to change its policies and practices.

Even more disturbing to UNHCR was the rapidly deteriorating asylum situation in Western Europe during this period. Previously, Western Europe had demonstrated a fairly liberal attitude towards asylum seekers and the Office had great influence on the majority of governments in the region. By the 1980s, however, Europe's welcoming policies towards asylum seekers had changed dramatically. The numbers of asylum applicants in European countries rose from 20,000 in 1976 to 158,000 in 1980. Governments reacted by tightening border controls, but such deterrent measures did not work for long. By the end of the 1980s, the numbers of asylum applications in Europe had reached some 450,000 a year.

From 1983 to 1989, some 60 percent of asylum seekers in Europe came from developing countries, driven by political crises and armed conflicts in Africa, Asia, and the Middle East. The influx included many people who, although they could not safely return to their home countries, did not meet the criteria of the 1951 Convention. The Iran–Iraq War of the mid-1980s generated 150,000 asylum applicants, civil wars in Sri Lanka brought 100,000 Tamils, and the war in Lebanon brought some 50,000 Lebanese to Europe. Growing numbers of economic migrants also tried to use the asylum system and began to enter Europe.

The arrival in the West of large numbers of people with a variety of claims to asylum severely jolted existing practices and overtaxed refugee status determination systems. In addition, the majority of applicants who were rejected for asylum remained in Europe, sometimes for several years, working through appeals procedures and putting a considerable strain on reception and integration facilities. Governments came to believe that the most effective way to limit asylum seekers was to prevent them from arriving in the first place. Consequently, Western European governments began to build barriers, first by revising immigration laws and asylum regulations and procedures, and second by adopting restrictive practices and deterrent measures to curb new arrivals. Nearly all governments introduced legislation to make access to their asylum procedures more difficult and began to withdraw most social benefits and work permits from asylum seekers.

UNHCR responded to these developments by increasing its monitoring of Western asylum policies and by issuing critical reports of its findings. Not only did Western governments bristle at what they perceived as UNHCR unhelpfulness and interference in their domestic affairs, they also sought to exclude the Office from their discussions about their asylum policies. UNHCR's authority and expertise on refugee and asylum issues no longer gave the Office the power and influence it had previously enjoyed in Europe. By the mid-1980s, European governments and UNHCR no longer had converging interests, and European governments initiated new intergovernmental and regional groups on coordinating asylum policy. Most of these groups reflected the growing restrictionist policies in the region and were closed to outside observers, including UNHCR. By the late 1980s, UNHCR was almost totally excluded from asylum policy discussions in Europe and its own authority and autonomy in the region had sunk to a new low.

Western states were not the only ones who were impatient with the demands placed upon them by the growing numbers of refugees. By the late 1970s, many Third World governments that had once welcomed and sheltered refugees, particularly during the era of anti-colonial struggles, were becoming inhospitable and hostile. An increasing number of refugees were unable to find safe haven in the developing world and were turned back at borders or forcibly repatriated. Mass inflows of refugees were seen to impose significant economic, environmental and political burdens on poor developing states and threaten domestic stability and central governmental authority. Consequently, many host states began to make their adherence to international refugee protection standards and practices conditional on increased international assistance and on greatly expanded overseas resettlement quotas from UNHCR and the donor community.

This situation was compounded by the intensification of the Cold War during the 1980s, which shifted the structure of the bipolar conflict across the entire developing world. As rivalry between the United States and the Soviet Union caused both powers to support local clients, internal conflicts became globalized and extremely violent.[19] Consequently, regional and intra-state conflicts in Indochina, Afghanistan, Central America, the Horn of Africa, and Southern Africa became prolonged and debilitating affairs, and generated large waves of refugees. As a result, the global refugee population tripled from 3 million in 1977 to over 10 million in 1982.

In light of such developments, refugee situations across the developing world became protracted and seemingly insoluble during the 1980s. The majority of refugees fleeing regional conflicts in Africa, Asia, and Central America were contained in refugee camps and provided with long-term care and maintenance. The international community failed to devise comprehensive or long-term political solutions or to provide any alternatives to prolonged camp existence, and finding solutions for these refugee situations became increasingly difficult. Solutions were further frustrated by armed groups that established themselves in refugee camps across the Third World. These groups often hid behind the humanitarian character of refugee camps and provided labor, military recruits and political legitimacy to the guerrilla resistance movements. These "refugee warrior" communities, such as the Afghan *mujahideen*, Cambodian Khmer Rouge, and Nicaraguan Contras, served as important instruments and proxies both in the interventionist policies of the external powers and in the regional power struggles.[20]

These refugee crises presented complex challenges to UNHCR as the Office found itself responding to massive refugee crises on three different continents simultaneously. Under Sadruddin's successor, Poul Hartling, UNHCR also found it difficult to maintain an impartial and humanitarian approach to its work. Virtually all of its funding came from Western governments who had a geopolitical interest in supporting UNHCR camps which housed anti-Communist "refugee warriors." As a result, Western donor governments were receptive to UNHCR appeals for assistance for a rapidly growing global refugee population, and the organization's annual budget consequently mushroomed from approximately US$76 million in 1975 to more than US $500 million in 1980.

Protracted refugee situations and the paucity of solutions

While UNHCR received substantial donor support for its programs in the Third World during the late 1970s and early 1980s, the politicization of refugee problems precluded the resolution of many refugee situations. UNHCR's three traditional solutions no longer proved adequate, as both geopolitics and local political realities frustrated efforts at repatriation, local integration and resettlement. By the mid-1980s, most overseas resettlement programs had dramatically reduced and Third World host governments restricted local integration to all but a few refugees. This lack of solutions meant that the majority of the world's refugees were given temporary asylum in camps, with no prospect of effective long-term solutions. A variety of interests converged during this period to maintain this status quo. The donor countries, particularly the US, generously funded most of these camps because they provided refuge for those displaced in regions of strategic importance to the West. During most of the 1980s, there was no political will on the part of the superpowers and their regional clients to seek political solutions to the longstanding regional conflicts. The confinement of refugees to remote border encampments removed any sense that there was an urgent need to address the root causes and press for political compromises and solutions. Host governments, concerned about the security risks of hosting refugees from neighboring countries and about the enormous strains on local economic, political, environmental, and physical resources, viewed camps as the most convenient way to segregate refugees and to limit their impact on local populations. UNHCR and NGO officials believed that by assembling refugees in one place they could better supply them with food and shelter and other basic necessities upon which their survival depended. Refugee camps also focused donor governments' attention and demonstrated a tangible proof of a real need. Even the refugees' own political leaders recognized the advantages of camp life as a way of keeping their cause before the world. Furthermore, the refugee warriors of Afghanistan, Cambodia, Central America, the Horn of Africa, Palestine and Southern Africa all maintained political solidarity in exile through the tight leadership structures possible in refugee camps.

The explosion of refugee numbers in the 1980s and the protracted nature of refugee situations eventually strained UNHCR's administrative and financial structures to breaking point. The global refugee total grew steadily from 10 million in 1980 to 17 million by the end of the decade. In the early 1980s, this surge in refugee numbers was matched by government contributions to UNHCR, but contributions soon failed to keep pace with the growing refugee numbers. The Office was also facing increasing competition from the NGO community for scarce donor resources. During the 1980s, the number of NGOs grew and assumed progressively greater responsibilities in providing assistance to refugees. At the same time, many of the UN agencies, including UNHCR, hampered by their mandates and by the political interests of donor states, were limited in their ability to respond to complex refugee situations. As a result, donor governments channeled more official funds through NGOs to high-profile relief programs, starting a trend that would continue to expand into the 1990s and the twenty-first century. Consequently, UNHCR found it increasingly difficult to continue to raise the money required to fully fund its expanding budget. In fact, UNHCR's funding per refugee fell by more than 50 percent in constant US dollars between 1980 and 1989.[21]

In an effort to respond to these challenges and to demonstrate UNHCR's relevance to the interests and priorities of donor governments, the new High Commissioner, Jean-Pierre Hocké, sought to shift the Office's focus from legal protection to material assistance operations, especially in the Third World. In his view, the traditional means and approaches of the Office no longer worked. He believed that UNHCR was too protection-oriented. Consequently, he elevated the operations and assistance side of UNHCR and downgraded the once powerful Department of International Protection. He advocated a new strategy for the developing world that required UNHCR to deal not only with asylum countries, as the Office was traditionally inclined to do, but also with countries of origin and with the "root causes" of refugee exoduses. In particular, the High Commissioner identified repatriation as UNHCR's new policy priority and as "the only realistic alternative to indefinite subsistence on charity"[22] and to protracted confinement in camps.

Hocké became High Commissioner at a time when there were no serious political negotiations underway to end the regional conflicts that had created the refugee crisis in the South.[23] Western governments were reluctant to offer resettlement to these refugees and Third World host governments were reluctant to offer refugees the opportunity to integrate with local populations. For Hocké, repatriation was the only viable alternative to the current situation and he vigorously began to promote return as the solution to protracted care and maintenance. In this effort, he had the backing of the Executive Committee which, during its October 1985 session, adopted a conclusion that encouraged the High Commissioner to look for opportunities to promote repatriation. These initiatives included promoting dialogue, acting as an intermediary, and facilitating communication between governments and refugees, but also actively pursuing return where there were appropriate conditions.

UNHCR subsequently began to play a more proactive role in repatriation and developed new thinking about repatriation and refugee protection. The Office's repatriation policies became more flexible and based more on pragmatic considerations and less on protection principles. Within the organization, there was a growing view that, with resettlement and local integration no longer realistic as solutions, refugees could not be satisfactorily protected in camps where they were increasingly exposed to physical harm. Rather, protection required freeing refugees from camps and finding a way for them to return to their home countries as quickly as possible, even if that occurred under less than ideal circumstances. The UNHCR Executive Committee discouraged the Office from waiting for opportunities to arise, but rather encouraged it to create the conditions that made repatriation possible. In the late 1980s, UNHCR actively promoted the repatriations of Tamils to Sri Lanka and of Salvadorans to El Salvador despite the fact that these policies posed considerable risks for returnees who returned in the midst of extremely violent civil wars.

Efforts to find comprehensive solutions: ICARA, CIREFCA and the Indochinese CPA

Other important initiatives during this period involved the use of development planning to address refugee situations in Africa and the formulation of comprehensive regional approaches to resolve the protracted refugee crises in Central America and Indochina. While each of these approaches varied in success, they contain important lessons about the role that UNHCR has been able to play in resolving protracted refugee situations and in responding to shifting regional and global political opportunities. In considering the development of these three regional approaches, it is important to be mindful of the fact that they were being developed and implemented almost simultaneously, and in light of the restrictions being placed on asylum in the North, as outlined above. Although, in practice, CIREFCA and the Indochinese CPA continued to be implemented during the 1990s, both are addressed in this chapter because they were developed as responses to prominent refugee movements associated with the geopolitics of the Cold War and because their implementation was largely made possible by the impetus created by the end of the Cold War.

During the 1960s and early 1970s, African states hosted an ever-growing number of refugees fleeing both wars of national liberation and conflict in post-colonial states. All regions of Africa were affected, and the total number of refugees in Africa reached 1 million by 1970. Many host states chose to accommodate these refugees through local settlement schemes. Under these schemes, refugees were provided with land for settlement and farming, received technical and financial support from the host state and international organizations, and were encouraged to become economically self-sufficient. Initially, this approach proved to be successful. By the late 1970s, however, the local settlement approach became unsustainable as the number of refugees in Africa continued to climb and refugee populations became increasingly dependent on international assistance to meet their basic needs.

In response to these concerns, the OAU sponsored a conference in 1979 to examine the particular problem of refugees in Africa. During the conference, many African governments stated that a new approach was necessary if they were to continue to provide such generous asylum to ever-increasing refugee populations. Moreover, they argued that greater support was required from donor states to help manage the adverse impact of refugees on the economies and environments of African host states. For their part, however, donor governments had expressed their reluctance to fund lengthy refugee assistance programs across the continent.

In an effort to overcome this impasse, African states used their growing influence in the General Assembly to push for additional resources for the assistance of host states in the early 1980s. In November 1980, the General Assembly passed a resolution that called for an

International Conference on Assistance to Refugees in Africa (ICARA), to be held the following year. The resolution recognized that Africa had come to host over half the world's refugees, and that the General Assembly was "aware of the consequent social and economic burden placed on African countries of asylum."[24]

The Conference, known as ICARA I, had three aims: (1) to focus world attention on Africa's refugee problem; (2) to mobilize additional resources for the problem; and, finally, (3) to assist host countries through the application of these additional resources. There is some disagreement over the extent to which ICARA I, held in Geneva in April 1981, fulfilled its objectives. The Conference did focus international attention on the scale of the refugee problem in Africa and mobilized more than US$570 million in pledges for African host states.[25] ICARA I also marked the introduction of the proposed use of development assistance to facilitate refugees' self-sufficiency and local integration, and consequently represents the start of UNHCR's "refugee aid and development" (RAD) approach.[26] That said, the Conference fell short of meeting the expectations of the organizers and African states. Most of the money pledged by donor states was heavily earmarked and directed to a limited number of popular host states, while relatively little was pledged to those host states that were deemed by the organizers to be most in need, such as Ethiopia and other countries in the Horn of Africa.

When the question of assistance to refugees in Africa returned to the agenda of the General Assembly in December 1982, it was noted that while ICARA I

> [had] succeeded in raising world consciousness about the plight of refugee and returnees in Africa, as well as the problems of asylum countries, the overall results of the Conference in terms of financial and material assistance have fallen short of the expectations of the African countries.[27]

The UN Secretary-General, in close cooperation with the OAU and UNHCR, was requested to convene a second International Conference on Assistance to Refugees in Africa (ICARA II) in 1984 to review the results of ICARA I, to consider providing "additional assistance to refugees and returnees in Africa," and

> to consider the impact imposed on the national economies of the African countries concerned and to provide them with required assistance to strengthen their social and economic infrastructure

to cope with the burden of dealing with large numbers of refugees and returnees.[28]

A rigorous process of consultation was established through which country reports were prepared for ICARA II, providing a detailed assessment of the assistance needs of refugees and returnees, in addition to the assistance required by host countries to develop the infrastructure necessary to better cope with the refugee burden. While the preparations for ICARA II were impressive, the response from donor countries was not. Many donor governments felt that ICARA I had been a success, and were consequently reluctant to participate in ICARA II.[29] Through ICARA II, it became clear that there were significant differences between host and donor countries on what burdens were to be borne by host states and how these should be addressed, notwithstanding the extensive preparatory work.

Although only US$81 million was pledged at the conference, there was optimism that ICARA II's Final Declaration and Program of Action set out generic principles that could be built upon, including the need for ongoing assistance, acknowledgment of Africa's disproportionate refugee burden, and the need to incorporate the needs of refugees in broader development planning.[30] The principles developed at ICARA II ultimately had little lasting practical legacy, however, and the additional financial contributions it raised were insignificant relative to the growing needs on the ground. As with ICARA I, the cause of failure was primarily a North–South polarization in expectations and interests, and a North–South division in the understanding of the purpose of the conference. While African states wished to focus on burden sharing and compensation for host states, donor states wished to focus on solutions for refugee situations. While donors did not reject the notion of expanded burden sharing *per se*, an increased economic commitment needed to be directly linked to expanded access to local integration. Given that UNHCR had conceived ICARA I and II more as one-off pledging conferences than as a political process, insufficient effort had gone into ensuring that these interests could be simultaneously met. Shortly after the end of the ICARA II conference in 1984, news broke of the massive famine affecting Ethiopia. Once international attention shifted from refugees to mobilizing humanitarian assistance in response to the Ethiopian famine, the initial momentum generated by ICARA was lost.

In contrast to UNHCR's efforts in Africa, the Office's response to the regional refugee crisis in Central America yielded more significant outcomes. The International Conference on Central American Refugees

(CIREFCA[31]) was an attempt to facilitate a cooperative international response to the massive and prolonged forced displacement caused by civil conflicts and brutal counter-insurgency campaigns in the region during the 1970s and 1980s.[32] The Conference, held in Guatemala City in 1989, adopted a Concerted Plan of Action to address the highly politicized issue of displacement in the region. While this plan represents the core of the initiative, CIREFCA was "conceived not only as an event, but, perhaps even more significantly, as a process."[33] Lasting from 1987 to 1994, and set within the wider context of the regional peace process at the end of the Cold War, it aimed to promote access to durable solutions for the region's refugees and displaced through an integrated development approach that built on the principles of Refugee Aid and Development.

CIREFCA was not only a follow-up to the 1984 Cartagena Declaration but also capitalized on the Esquipulas II peace deal for Central America, concluded in August 1987. It was evident from the beginning of the Central American peace negotiations that a successful resolution of the region's conflicts would involve not only the end of the various conflicts but also large-scale assistance in the wake of the widespread social and economic disruption that the wars had produced, including the displacement of peoples. Hence, the Esquipulas II peace agreement took the position that a lasting peace could not be achieved without initiatives to solve the problems of refugees, displaced persons, and returnees throughout the region. UNHCR drew on this specific reference to the needs of uprooted people and channeled it into a regional and international commitment to finding solutions for the displaced.

Also significant was the close link between humanitarian and development actors in the process, especially through the incorporation of the CIREFCA Concerted Plan of Action into UNDP's wider post-conflict reconstruction initiative in the region. In fact, the underlying ethos of CIREFCA was to find durable solutions for displacement through an integrated development approach, closing the "gap" between relief and development to simultaneously address the needs of refugees, returnees, and the internally displaced, while also benefiting local communities. UNHCR and UNDP jointly ran a permanent secretariat for the initiative in San José, Costa Rica. Both organizations provided regional states with technical support in developing their own "priority projects," both for initial submission to CIREFCA and for submission to the International Follow-Up Conferences.

The process involved the participation of countries of asylum and countries of origin in the region as well as donor governments and international organizations. The project proposals varied from country to country, depending notably on whether the state was primarily a country of origin or asylum. When considering countries of asylum, further weight was given to how tolerant or restrictive that country was towards freedom of movement and the socio-economic integration of refugees. For example, in Mexico, the projects focused on self-reliance for Guatemalan refugees, notably through agricultural projects in Chiapas and the rural resettlement projects in Campeche and Quintana Roo. In Honduras, given the state's restrictions on freedom of movement, attention was paid to strengthening UNHCR assistance in camps, pending return to Guatemala and Nicaragua. In El Salvador, aside from nominal support for Nicaraguan refugees and returnees, primary attention was given to meeting the basic needs of the country's IDPs.

In its immediate aftermath, CIREFCA was generally seen as a success in terms of enhancing refugees' access to protection and durable solutions.[34] In total, CIREFCA is estimated to have channeled US $422.3 million in additional resources to the region. Throughout the process, the most significant group of donors was the European states, both bilaterally and through the European Economic Community (EEC). The process has also been widely credited with helping to consolidate peace in Central America.

Although there has been little formal monitoring of the projects implemented under CIREFCA, its success can be attributed to a number of features. First, CIREFCA was based upon a collaborative approach, involving a range of other UN actors. Rather than being conceived in isolation, CIREFCA was structurally connected to the wider peace and post-conflict reconstruction initiatives for the region. UNHCR also developed a well-defined partnership with UNDP in order to implement its integrated development approach to promoting self-reliance, local integration, and repatriation. Second, UNHCR provided political leadership. Rather than being conceived as a technocratic pledging conference, UNHCR developed a sustained political process, helping to channel states' wider interests into a commitment to refugee protection and durable solutions. Similar approaches were used by UNHCR in responding to the needs of millions of refugees from Vietnam, Laos, and Cambodia.

The international response to the Indochinese crisis in 1989 brought to an end one of the most longstanding refugee problems confronting UNHCR and the international community from the mid-1970s to the mid-1990s. The consolidation of Communist South-East Asian regimes in 1975 resulted in an estimated 3 million people fleeing Vietnam,

Cambodia, and Laos in the following two decades. Laotians and Cambodians fled overland to neighboring Thailand. Most Vietnamese fled in small boats, and many died in shipwrecks or were targeted by pirates. Humanitarianism, coupled with the geopolitical interests of the United States, motivated Western states to recognize the "boat people" as refugees *prima facie* and to resettle them. More than 550,000 Indochinese sought asylum in South-East Asia between 1975 and 1979 alone, of which 200,000 were resettled to Western countries.[35]

As the arrival of Vietnamese boat people continued to exceed resettlement quotas, regional states declared in June 1979 that the scale of the crisis exceeded their ability to respond, and that they were no longer willing to accept new arrivals. This reluctance, and reports of regional states pushing boats carrying asylum seekers away from their shores, led to an International Conference on Indochinese Refugees in July 1979. States agreed that worldwide resettlement quotas would be doubled, that the boat people would be recognized as refugees *prima facie*, that illegal departures would be prevented, and that regional processing centers would be established. The result was a formalized *quid pro quo*; resettlement to Western states in exchange for assurances of first asylum in the region.

The agreement resulted in over one million Indochinese refugees being given temporary asylum in South-East Asia and then resettled in the West between 1979 and 1988. However, by the end of 1988 the number of people fleeing Vietnam was increasing, and the willingness of both host states in the region to offer protection and of third countries beyond the region to offer resettlement was declining. With resettlement quotas declining, there was a growing pool of "long-stayers" in first asylum camps and the countries in the region began to identify resettlement as a "pull factor" attracting growing numbers of economic migrants. Despite the large numbers resettled since 1979, roughly the same number of Vietnamese refugees (150,000) remained in camps in South-East Asia at the end of 1988 as there had been in 1979.[36] In the words of Sergio Vieira de Mello, Director of UNHCR's Asia Bureau at the time, there was therefore a need for "a new solutions-oriented consensus involving the cooperation of countries of origin, first asylum and resettlement."[37]

In the late 1980s, the Socialist Republic of Vietnam (SRV) declared itself willing to engage in the process and to repatriate, without punishment or persecution, those who voluntarily agreed to return.[38] This shift stood in stark contrast to its position since 1975, and was widely seen as part its wider efforts at rapprochement with states in the region. More generally, this rapprochement was pursued in the context of improved relations between the superpowers at the end of the Cold War and progress on resolving the conflict in Cambodia, including the withdrawal of Vietnamese troops. The willingness of the SRV to accept the return of its nationals opened the possibility of conducting refugee status determination as a screening mechanism to exclude from resettlement those not found to have a well-founded fear of persecution in their country of origin.[39] This new element offered the prospect of possible return to Vietnam and provided the basis for a new consensus on international cooperation in relation to Indochinese refugees.

The Indochinese Comprehensive Plan of Action (CPA), adopted in Geneva in 1989, relied upon a three-way commitment by countries of first asylum in the region, the main country of origin, and resettlement countries.[40] Countries of first asylum in the region re-committed themselves to the principle of temporary asylum, pending a solution elsewhere. Vietnam, as the main country of origin, agreed not only to facilitate the return of those found not to be eligible for refugee status, but also to manage an "orderly departure program" for those fleeing the country. For their part, resettlement states agreed to resettle all those who had arrived in countries of first asylum up to a certain date, and to resettle all those who arrived after the cut-off date and were determined to be refugees by individual status determination.

By 1996, the camps and detention centers in the region had been cleared in accordance with the CPA and the issue of the Vietnamese "boat people" was finally resolved. The CPA has often been criticized by human rights advocates, especially given concerns relating to the forcible return of those "screened out" and the conditions of detention in countries of first asylum. Despite these criticisms, the CPA is seen to have generally achieved its objectives of reducing the number of clandestine departures and finding extra-regional durable solutions for recognized refugees. In 1989, roughly 70,000 Vietnamese sought asylum in South-East Asia. By 1992, this number had fallen to 41. At the same time, over 1,950,000 refugees had been resettled by the end of the CPA in 1995; 1,250,000 to the United States alone. On this basis, the CPA is seen by many as a success, and an unprecedented example of UNHCR successfully facilitating inter-state political agreement in order to overcome a longstanding mass exodus.

While the Indochinese CPA and CIREFCA were initiated at the end of the 1980s, they did not come to fruition until the 1990s. Until the late 1980s, Cold War politics continued to paralyze diplomatic initiatives to break the deadlock of regional conflicts in most of Africa, Asia, and Central America and hence most refugees were destined to remain trapped in camps for most of the decade. Consequently, UNHCR's care and maintenance programs, staff and budget continued to grow inexorably to care for the world's protracted refugee situations. The Office was also funding new emergencies in Somalia, Mozambique, and Sudan, continuing outflows from Afghanistan, Iran, and Vietnam and expensive large-scale repatriation programs in Namibia, Nicaragua, and Sri Lanka, which included not only emergency relief but also reintegration and development projects. By the end of the decade, UNHCR's budget was in serious deficit. Consequently, donor governments forced High Commissioner Hocké to resign and placed the organization under their strict financial control. These events highlighted what remains the most significant institutional weakness of the Office, namely its dependence on voluntary contributions to carry out its program.

The financial and institutional crisis at UNHCR coincided with a dramatic shift in the international political environment that occurred with the winding down of the Cold War and the collapse of the Soviet Union and Communist regimes in Eastern Europe. The post-Cold War era would generate massive new numbers of refugees and displaced people and would pose difficult new challenges for UNHCR and the international community. These challenges include involvement for the first time in providing assistance and protection to displaced people in countries of refugee origin, growing international recognition and importance of IDPs, the continuing problem of protracted refugee situations, the attempt to strengthen asylum protection by reaffirming the relevance of the 1951 Convention, and the need to respond to changes in transnational migration flows. The tension between UNHCR's normative agenda and the security interests of states consequently sharpened following the end of the Cold War and the global governance of refugee protection and assistance became increasingly complex.

3 UNHCR in the post-Cold War era

The 1990s ushered in momentous changes in international politics. At the close of the 1980s, the flood of refugees from East to West Germany helped bring down the Berlin Wall, expedited the unification of the two German states, and generated the most significant transformation in international relations since the Second World War. By 1991, the Soviet Union had also collapsed and cut off its financial support to its client regimes throughout the Third World. As the decades-old confrontation between the United States and the Soviet Union came to an abrupt end, many of the political obstacles to settling the protracted conflicts of the Cold War decreased considerably. The political transformations taking place in the developing world at the end of the Cold War gave UNHCR an unprecedented opportunity to resolve some of the world's most longstanding refugee situations.

While the end of the Cold War engendered calls for a "new world order," dramatic changes in global and regional politics during the 1990s presented new challenges for UNHCR. The optimism that characterized the end of the Cold War quickly evaporated as the international community failed to effectively respond to a number of new crises, including the collapse of Somalia, the break-up of the former Yugoslavia and genocide in Rwanda. Each of these crises witnessed significant and complex dynamics of forced displacement, and UNHCR was called upon to play a more prominent role. By engaging more directly in debates on new sources of national, regional, and international insecurity and by retooling itself to provide humanitarian assistance in intra-state conflicts, the Office sought to encourage sustained international action on behalf of refugees. Instead, governments used humanitarian relief as a substitute for political action to address the root causes of mass displacement. At the same time, states in the global North and South adopted a series of increasingly restrictive asylum policies aimed to keep refugee problems at arm's length, thereby frustrating efforts to find solutions for longstanding refugee situations. The advent of the "war on terror" following the attacks on the US on 11 September 2001 exacerbated states' security concerns and ushered in a new era of restrictions against refugees and further challenges for UNHCR and its mandate. Over the past 15 years, the Office has consequently tried to adapt its work to be effective in a global political context that is significantly different from the one in which it was created. As this chapter illustrates, however, this process of adaptation has had significant implications for UNHCR's interpretation of its mandate and the future direction of the organization. This chapter begins by examining UNHCR's changing role during the 1990s: its growing role in repatriation, its response to new intra-state conflicts, and the expansion of its work to include a greater role in humanitarian relief and IDP protection. The second half of the chapter explores UNHCR's work in the early twenty-first century, including how it has responded to a range of challenges including the new security environment of the so-called "war on terror," new conflicts in Iraq and Darfur, and humanitarian reform across the UN system.

The 1990s: "the decade of repatriation"

Building on the opportunities created by the end of the Cold War, the new High Commissioner, Sadako Ogata (1990–2000), made repatriation a primary objective for UNHCR shortly after she assumed office in 1990.[1] Continuing a policy direction initiated in the mid-1980s, Ogata declared that the 1990s would be "the decade of voluntary repatriation." Indeed, massive numbers of refugees and displaced people did return home in the early to mid-1990s. More than 42,000 refugees returned to Namibia following a UN-brokered peace settlement. After years of war and famine, up to one million refugees returned to Ethiopia and Eritrea after the change of government in Addis Ababa in 1991. In 1992 and 1993, approximately 370,000 Cambodians repatriated from camps in Thailand, where many had been living since 1979. Between 1992 and 1996, some 1.7 million Mozambican refugees returned to their homeland from Malawi and five other neighboring states. Despite the outbreak of civil conflict in Afghanistan and the absence of a central government, more than 2.7 million Afghans repatriated from Pakistan and Iran during the period from 1992 to 1996. Around the world, UNHCR estimates that more than 9 million refugees repatriated between 1991 and 1996. This total represents a substantial increase over the period from 1985 to 1990 when only about 1.2 million refugees repatriated.[2]

UNHCR was also confronted with the challenge of addressing refugee situations where the end of the Cold War did not bring peace in the country of origin. Indeed, not all Cold War conflicts were easily resolved, as conflict persisted in countries such as Angola and Afghanistan and other political and economic obstacles proved insurmountable. At the same time, the early 1990s saw the emergence of new conflicts in countries such as Liberia, Iraq, Sierra Leone, Somalia, the former Yugoslavia, Rwanda and East Timor. In order to facilitate the return of refugees, even to situations where the conflict continued, UNHCR acquired new means for considering repatriation under less demanding standards. The Office developed terminology and concepts such as "safe return," which stipulated that conditions in the home country did not have to improve "substantially" but only "appreciably" so that there could be a "safe" return.[3] Repatriation no longer had to be a strictly voluntary decision by refugees to return home. Rather, it would now be UNHCR who could make the assessment as to whether conditions presented a threat to their safety. Moreover, there was a growing view that refugee safety did not necessarily always outweigh the security interests of states or broader peacebuilding and conflict resolution objectives.[4]

A more proactive policy on repatriation also required UNHCR to become involved in countries of origin, supplementing its traditional protection activities with work in the reintegration, rehabilitation, and development processes of returnee areas. Since a growing number of refugees were repatriating under some form of pressure into situations of social unrest and political instability, UNHCR felt there was need for an international presence to monitor the welfare of the returnees and to facilitate their reintegration back into their home societies. Moreover, there was international concern that since most refugees were returning to areas that had been devastated by decades of conflict, they would be unable to support themselves and might once again be displaced.

To fill the gap between short-term humanitarian relief and long-term development, UNHCR initiated a new strategy of "returnee aid and development."[5] This strategy envisioned UNHCR providing short-term assistance to promote reintegration and that this would be followed up with long-term development assistance supplied by international development agencies. But international development and financial institutions perceived themselves as having a development, not a displacement, focus. Hence, UNDP and the World Bank were not disposed to develop economic development programs in returnee-populated areas and worked too slowly to handle the transition from conflict to peace and from emergency relief to development. To fill this emerging gap, a great deal of UNHCR's energy and resources were increasingly devoted to promoting post-conflict reintegration. In this way, the early post-Cold War period saw UNHCR take steps to further expand the scope of its mandate to respond to the evolving needs of refugees and returnees.

Responding to humanitarian emergencies in intra-state conflicts

While UNHCR tried to resolve the long-standing refugee problems of the previous decade primarily through repatriation programs, the Office was faced with responding to a vast number of new large-scale humanitarian emergencies.[6] Most major refugee crises of the 1990s were triggered by conflicts in which ethnic identity was a prominent element in both the goals and methods of adversaries. In such conflicts, including those following the break-up of the former Yugoslavia, the forced displacement of civilian populations was a primary objective. Civilians were increasingly targeted as large-scale internal displacements became a political strategy in claiming control over territory. In other conflicts, such as in Myanmar (Burma), central governments sought to counter political opposition through counter-insurgency campaigns, including campaigns of forced displacement to deny insurgents the support of the local population. Thus, refugee movements and other instances of forced displacement during the early 1990s were increasingly the result of both communal conflicts and human rights abuses, all fuelled by the increasing availability of arms in the aftermath of the Cold War.

As instances of conflict multiplied, UNHCR had to confront refugee emergencies in rapid, sometimes overlapping, succession. Refugee crises in Iraq, Bosnia, Croatia, Somalia, Myanmar, Bhutan, the Caucasus, Tajikistan, Rwanda, Burundi, Liberia, Sierra Leone, the Democratic Republic of Congo, Kosovo, and East Timor strained the capacities of the organization almost to breaking point.[7] By 1996, the number of refugees in the world totaled 13.2 million and the cost of UNHCR's operations had risen from around US$550 million in 1990 to about US$1.3 billion in 1996.

The plight of IDPs also emerged as an international issue in the early 1990s.[8] As the number of intra-state conflicts proliferated, the number of IDPs rapidly rose. In 1982, it was estimated that there were 1.2 million IDPs in the world. By 1992, the number had risen to 24 million.[9] While the dramatic rise in the number of IDPs prompted international concern, the political issues surrounding IDPs, particularly state sovereignty, made the issue of IDPs one of the most complex problems confronting the international community. The challenges of responding to the rise in IDP emergencies was compounded by the fact that there existed no adequate body of international law to regulate the treatment of IDPs by governments and no specific international organization mandated to assist and protect them. In fact, IDPs fell between the gaps of existing mandates of the different UN agencies.

The proliferation of humanitarian emergencies and the rising importance of IDPs in the 1990s prompted several efforts to reform the UN's emergency response capacity and humanitarian institutions. In an attempt to create a focal point for IDPs within the UN system, the UN Secretary-General, Boutros Ghali, appointed Francis Deng as his representative for internally displaced persons in 1992. More generally, the General Assembly created the Department of Humanitarian Affairs (DHA) and appointed the UN's first humanitarian assistance coordinator in March 1992 in an effort to strengthen the coordination of emergency humanitarian assistance. At the same time, the Inter-Agency Standing Committee (IASC) was established to facilitate inter-agency coordination in humanitarian emergencies. The DHA, however, was never given adequate authority over other UN agencies or adequate funding to carry out its functions. Moreover, other agencies, including UNHCR, were wary of the DHA becoming increasingly active in the field, directly competing with their own authority and programs.

Subsequent attempts to reform the UN humanitarian structure revealed continuing tensions among the UN humanitarian agencies. In response, the DHA was eliminated in a major restructuring of the UN system in 1997 under Secretary-General Kofi Annan. Annan established a new position of Under-Secretary-general for Humanitarian Affairs (USG) and renamed the DHA the Office for the Coordination of Humanitarian Affairs (OCHA). The USG now acts as both the head of OCHA and as the Emergency Relief Coordinator (ERC) that chairs the IASC. In addition, the USG serves as the Chair of the Executive Committee for Humanitarian Affairs, which provides a means to integrate the various components involved in humanitarian emergencies: humanitarian relief, human rights, political affairs, and peacekeeping.

NGOs also played an increasingly important operational role in humanitarian emergencies during the 1990s.[10] In 1994, NGOs delivered an estimated 10–14 percent of total international aid, more than the entire UN system combined (excluding the World Bank and the International Monetary Fund). By the mid-1990s, 20 percent of US aid was directed through NGOs. By the end of the decade, the majority of the US humanitarian aid budget, particularly in high profile emergencies like Kosovo, was channeled to NGOs through bilateral programs.

Changing understandings of international security and UNHCR's response

Another important feature of the post-Cold War period was the significant change in understandings of the sources of threats to national and international security and the range of new security issues identified by states. Speaking at the first summit-level meeting at the end of the Cold War, the President of the Security Council noted in 1992 that "the non-military sources of instability in the economic, social, humanitarian and ecological fields have become threats to international peace and security."[11] In particular, refugee crises assumed a new degree of political salience in the discourse about global and regional security.[12] Refugee movements were central elements of numerous Security Council resolutions and were the subject of increasing discussion in political and military fora such as the Security Council, the North Atlantic Treaty Organization, and regional organizations.[13]

During this period, there was also a marked shift in attitude towards intervention in the domestic affairs of other states, particularly in situations where governments were unwilling or unable to respond to massive displacements within their own borders.[14] In many international political and security crises, refugees were viewed as posing threats to regional and international security, and thus providing a basis for action under Chapter VII of the UN Charter.[15] In Northern Iraq, Somalia, the former Yugoslavia, and Haiti, international intervention was authorized in response to refugee flows. Moreover, forced displacements were also at the center of crises in the Great Lakes region, West Africa, the Balkans, and East Timor. In most of these cases, the UN, or regional or national forces acting with UN authorization, attempted to tackle crises leading to mass displacement by directly intervening in intra-state conflicts.

At the same time that refugees came to be viewed as possibly posing threats to international and regional security, refugees were perceived increasingly by host states as burdens as threats to social cohesion. In the face of the growing numbers of illegal migrants and the abuse of asylum systems, the trend of increasingly restrictive asylum policies that began in the 1980s gathered pace. Governments in the North became increasingly reluctant to grant asylum and enacted severe new entry controls. In place of asylum, Western states introduced various forms of "temporary protection" to deal with those fleeing war and "ethnic cleansing." For developing countries, the growing numbers of displaced people entering already precarious or failing economies presented problems that threatened domestic stability and governmental authority. In many parts of the South, diminishing donor government support for long-term refugee assistance, coupled with declining levels of development assistance and the imposition of structural adjustment programs on many poorer and less stable states, contributed to the growing hostility towards refugees.

In response to these global developments, most governments not only introduced more restrictive asylum policies but also pushed for a comprehensive international policy which sought to contain refugee movements in regions of refugee origin through conflict resolution, peacemaking, and peacekeeping. These policies focused on preventing refugee flows, facilitating speedy repatriation, and assisting IDPs so as to prevent them from seeking asylum abroad. At the same time, the rise in global media attention to humanitarian emergencies put pressure on governments to respond. Governments therefore repeatedly tasked UNHCR and NGOs to provide emergency relief aid with a view towards alleviating, preventing, or containing refugee crises within their own country or region of origin. For the world's most powerful states, the provision of humanitarian assistance was financially and politically preferable to intervention as it satisfied public demands for some kind of action to alleviate human suffering while excusing governments from taking more decisive and risky forms of political and military intervention.

The fundamental changes in states' attitudes towards security at the end of the Cold War presented UNHCR with an opportunity to make itself more relevant to the international community. To demonstrate its relevance, the Office began to present its own work more in terms of contributing to regional and international peace and security. UNHCR believed that by appealing to states' security concerns it could convince policy-makers to direct political and financial resources towards finding solutions to refugee and IDP situations. The Office became more frequently involved in intra-state conflicts and in sharing responsibility with UN-mandated military forces in the assistance of displaced people within their own home countries. UNHCR also demonstrated a greater interest in preventing refugee flows, containing them, and finding solutions to the political problems that created mass flight. By emphasizing the responsibilities of refugee-sending states and by labeling the mass exodus of refugees as a threat to international peace and security, UNHCR sought to legitimize its own actions to facilitate repatriations as well as interventions by the UN and states into regions of refugee origin to alleviate or even solve the causes of flight.

The high priority given to humanitarian operations and the increasing recognition of a link between refugees, internal displacement and international security meant that UNHCR played an increasingly important role in placing refugees on the international political agenda.[16] Ogata energized the organization, and UNHCR became the central actor in many of the humanitarian crises of the 1990s. From 1992 on, the High Commissioner delivered regular reports to international and regional organizations on the potentially destabilizing effects of refugee and displacement crises. In the Balkans crises, the High Commissioner chaired the Humanitarian Issues Working Group of the International Conference on the Former Yugoslavia and regularly met international peace negotiators, government leaders, and leaders of the warring factions. Ogata also highlighted the potentially destabilizing consequences of displacement in numerous briefings to the Security Council, most notably in 1998 when she reported that the cycle of violence and repression by Serbian forces in Kosovo would lead to large-scale displacement.[17] For a High Commissioner, Ogata had unusual access to prime ministers, presidents and their foreign ministers and tried to use this access as a tool of persuasion and leverage.

The emergence of a new international security environment and a more assertive Security Council dramatically changed the way in which UNHCR operated. During the Cold War, in-country assistance and protection of IDPs and victims of war were perceived to violate state sovereignty and therefore were taboo for UN agencies. In the post-Cold War period, by contrast, the UN developed a series of new measures, including a number of humanitarian interventions, for responding to instances of forced displacement within intra-state conflicts. These initiatives included the offer of temporary protection rather than full refugee status, the establishment of safe havens, cross-border deliveries of assistance, and the use of military resources for the delivery of humanitarian assistance. For UNHCR, the major change in the handling of refugee issues included an increased focus on working in countries of origin—even in countries at war—to reduce the likelihood of massive refugee flows across borders. In addition, UNHCR was also frequently asked to take part in comprehensive and integrated UN peacekeeping or peacemaking operations that involved cooperation with political and military actors of the UN as well as with dozens, even hundreds, of NGOs.

In response to these dramatic developments, UNHCR expanded its services to a much wider range of people who were in need of assistance.

For example, "war-affected populations"—people who had not been uprooted but needed humanitarian assistance and protection—comprised a substantial proportion of UNHCR's beneficiary population during the height of the Bosnian conflict in the 1990s. As a result, the numbers of displaced people and war-affected populations receiving UNHCR assistance increased dramatically. Worldwide, the number of people receiving UNHCR assistance increased from 15 million in 1990 to a peak of 26 million in 1996. Significantly, refugees constituted only about 50 percent of this "population of concern" to UNHCR. As a result, UNHCR expanded from an organization focused exclusively on refugees into the UN's foremost humanitarian agency, thereby gaining a higher profile in international politics and securing more generous funding for its operations.[18]

Disillusionment with the new security initiatives and the rise of "Human Security"

By the mid-1990s, however, it became evident that these innovative methods of protection and assistance had not been derived from a clearly defined strategy, but had been developed in response to immediate security crises. As seemingly intractable conflicts continued in the Balkans, Africa and the former Soviet Union, it was apparent that states lacked the will to initiate effective enforcement to maintain peace and security, to empower human rights mechanisms, or to promote sustainable development in crisis regions. The major powers had only minimal interest in most intra-state conflicts and humanitarian crises, and international responses to refugee crises remained more often than not reactive, self-interested, and based on *ad hoc* initiatives. There was no guarantee that states would intervene in situations where it was desperately needed, as illustrated by the failure of the international community to respond to mass human rights violations in Rwanda and the former Yugoslavia. Bruised by their failure to restore stability in Somalia, the United States, the world's major governments and the UN chose to do nothing in the face of the 1994 Rwandan genocide. Similar concerns prevented Western governments from committing sufficient ground forces to Bosnia with an enforcement mission to defend the "safe areas," including Srebrenica.

Most alarmingly, the new initiatives also seemed to exacerbate and prolong the suffering of displaced people caught up in brutal conflicts. UNHCR's high-profile relief efforts in Northern Iraq, Bosnia, and Rwanda dramatically underlined the inadequacy of providing protection in humanitarian relief programs in the midst of on-going civil conflicts and regional security crises. Unlike its previous work in countries of asylum during most of the Cold War, UNHCR now had to work with governments and opposition movements and guerrilla factions, often in the context of collapsing states and where population displacement was among the central objectives of war. UNHCR often found itself ill-equipped to respond to the needs of IDPs and returnees who lived amid conditions of inter-communal violence and on-going conflict. Protecting civilians against reprisals and forced displacement, evacuating and relocating civilians from conflict areas and assisting besieged populations, such as those in Sarajevo, were new activities for most UNHCR staff. Most staff were neither recruited nor trained to work in the cross-fire of intra-state conflicts where soldiers and guerrillas viewed the internally displaced and returnees as the enemy, and UN assistance to these populations as an act of war.

As it tried to respond to the rapidly evolving nature of conflict and displacement in the post-Cold War world, UNHCR felt let down by the international community. This was especially true in the Great Lakes region of Central Africa. The failure to halt the genocide in Rwanda in 1994, the failure to halt the militarization of refugee camps in Zaire in 1994–1996, the failure to prevent the forced repatriation of Rwandan refugees in 1996, and the failure to protect and assist the Rwandan refugees driven into eastern Zaire from late 1996 onward vividly demonstrated for UNHCR the lack of commitment on the part of states to address the underlying causes of conflict in order to find solutions to refugee problems. The international community was all too often content to encourage UNHCR and other humanitarian organizations to deal with the consequences of conflicts rather than to actively engage in seeking political and security solutions in intra-state wars. The organization was often left to deal with impossible situations over which it had little control. It became clear to UNHCR that it could not resolve refugee situations on its own, but that refugee problems could only be resolved with the active and sustained involvement of the international community.

For their part, the major powers, particularly the United States, believed that the interventions of the early 1990s had overextended the UN, and that future interventions should be much more limited and essentially restricted to the most strategically important areas of the world. As Kofi Annan acknowledged in his annual report to the General Assembly in 1999, "the failure to intervene was driven more by the reluctance of Member States to pay the human and other costs of intervention, and by doubts that the use of force would be successful, than by concerns about sovereignty."[19] The use of armed force to stem refugee movements remained highly controversial within the international community.[20] The NATO intervention in Kosovo in 1999, as well as the bitter debates over Iraq in 2003, demonstrated that there exist significant objections, particularly among the developing states, to the concept of intervention and to the use of force to resolve security threats, much less refugee crises.

Throughout her term as High Commissioner, Sadako Ogata stressed that her most important challenge was how to strike a balance between the principles of refugee protection and the legitimate concerns of states.[21] However, the disastrous protection crises of the Great Lakes and other operations demonstrated for UNHCR that this balance could not be achieved solely through appealing to the security interests of states. UNHCR had overestimated the extent to which the international community was willing, and able, to intervene in sovereign states to aid refugees and displaced people. It also became clear that the security interests of states were narrower and more self-interested than UNHCR had anticipated, and were not always compatible with the protection needs of refugees.

In response, UNHCR toned down the political elements of its security discourse, redefined security by giving it a more humanitarian emphasis, and developed new concepts and operational tools.[22] In particular, it drew upon the notion of "human security," first introduced by UNDP in 1994,[23] and later incorporated into the foreign policy agendas of states such as Canada, Sweden, and Norway. The concept of human security represented an attempt to make the individual human being, rather than the nation-state, the main referent object for security. It symbolized a post-Cold War shift away from the previous global consensus on the inviolability of state sovereignty towards a growing recognition that sovereignty was at least partly conditional on ensuring that citizens had access to human rights and human development. UNHCR began to use the concept from the mid-1990s as a way to reconcile the security concerns of states, the protection needs of refugees, and the security needs of its staff. By drawing on the concept of human security, UNHCR sought to demonstrate that the real security of states and the international community could only be achieved by providing security for "people."[24]

However, the concept of human security proved to have a number of significant limitations. The emphasis of international law and international relations remained centered on state sovereignty and the promotion of state interests rather than on the safety and security of individuals, including refugees. While human security emphasized the links between human rights, physical security of individuals and the security of states, it was so all-encompassing a concept that it did not provide UNHCR with a very useful tool with which to understand and explain the nature of refugee problems.[25] The concept also did not adequately address the disjuncture between UNHCR's emphasis on human rights and the security concerns of states affected by disruptive refugee movements. In particular, human security underplayed or ignored the security concerns of states, especially the long-term consequences of hosting large numbers of refugees. It also focused on forced migration as a consequence of conflict, but ignored the fact that refugees can frequently be the cause of conflict. Consequently, human security, as defined by UNHCR, had a questionable utility as a framework for understanding the relationship between state security concerns, and refugee protection.

After the Great Lakes disaster, the international community began to debate a more structured response to address the security threats of hosting refugees, particularly the threat posed by the presence of armed elements in refugee camps.[26] In 1998, the Security Council adopted Resolution 1208, which outlined the responsibility of states, regional organizations, and the UN when responding to the security implications of refugee movements.[27] Then, in April 2000, the Security Council requested the Secretary-General to bring to its attention incidents involving the militarization of refugee camps and to consider taking "appropriate steps to create a secure environment for civilians endangered by conflicts."[28] A year later, UN Secretary-General Kofi Annan recognized the need for a military force to keep armed combatants out of refugee settlements and recommended that the Security Council deploy "international military observers to monitor the situation in camps for internally displaced persons and refugees when the presence of arms, combatants and armed elements is suspected ... [and] consider the range of options ... [including] compelling disarmament of the combatants or armed elements."[29]

Building on these discussions, UNHCR proposed a "ladder of options"—ranging from contingency planning and preventive measures through monitoring and policing to forceful intervention under Chapter VII of the UN Charter—as the foundation for a new UN policy response to the problems of insecurity in refugee camps.[30] Subsequently, UNHCR established stand-by arrangements with a limited number of governments for the provision of police and public security experts, who were designated as Humanitarian Security Officers (HSOs), to be deployed as part of UNHCR's Emergency Response teams at the beginning of refugee crises and would work with public security institutions of receiving countries. UNHCR also enhanced its own emergency response mechanism by participating in numerous civil-military conferences, designing training programs for HSOs, and establishing a focal point with the UN Security Coordinator (UNSECORD). Finally, UNHCR entered into discussions with the UN Department of Peacekeeping Operations (DPKO) regarding the possible deployment of missions to situations in which refugee-populated areas have become militarized or where they run the risk of falling under the control of groups suspected of genocide or crimes against humanity. However, such measures would prove ineffective in protecting refugees and displaced people in situations like Darfur or Somalia, where UNHCR or peacekeeping forces had little control.

UNHCR in the early twenty-first century

When Sadako Ogata departed as High Commissioner at the end of 2000, UNHCR faced a critical juncture. The Office had been widely criticized for its lack of preparedness and slow response to the 1999 refugee crisis in Kosovo, and the organization faced another severe financial crisis by the end of the decade. UNHCR's global stretch consequently receded and the organization assumed a more modest role in international security and international politics under the new High Commissioner, Ruud Lubbers (2001–2005). The work of UNHCR was further affected by a number of new trends that emerged in the early years of the twenty-first century, especially the dramatic fall in the level of armed conflict. From a very high level of civil or intra-state conflicts in the early 1990s, the number of these conflicts had decreased by some 40 percent by 2005. Consequently, there were fewer refugee emergencies than during the 1990s, and large numbers of refugees returned home as several acute conflicts were resolved. The number of refugees worldwide consequently declined from nearly 18 million in 1992 to just over 9 million at the beginning of 2005.

Despite these encouraging trends, Lubbers' term as High Commission began with the widespread acknowledgement of a crisis in the global refugee regime. Not only was there a serious shortfall in funding for UNHCR's budget, but host states in both the North and South continued to place restrictions on the asylum they offered to refugees. Combined with the inability of the international community to address persistent conflict and human rights abuses in "failed and fragile states," the restrictive policies of host states meant that a number of significant and longstanding refugee problems remained unresolved. An increasing proportion of the world's refugees remained in a protracted state of limbo, with no foreseeable solution to their plight. By 2004, some two-thirds of the world's refugees were trapped in protracted refugee situations.

Then, only nine months into Lubbers's term, the terrorist attacks on the United States on 11 September 2001 and the inauguration of the "war on terror" led to a further deterioration of refugee protection by states. The fight against terrorism created an unprecedented level of suspicion and hostility against refugees and migrants around the world. Most governments, especially those in Europe and North America, introduced stringent new anti-terrorist laws or gave new life to old laws once used to suppress peaceful dissent and other civil and political liberties. Politicians and the media began to portray all border-crossers, whether migrants or refugees, as potential terrorists and security threats. With each new terrorist attack, governments used security as a rationale to further tighten their immigration systems and visa regimes and limit their resettlement programs. As a result, the prospects for refugee protection declined precipitously in the years after September 2001.

As access to legal migration was limited, increasing numbers of both asylum seekers and migrants turned to the same trafficking channels to evade controls at border crossings and claim asylum in Western countries. It thus became increasingly difficult to distinguish between those in need of international protection and those moving in search of better economic opportunities. This phenomenon, known as the asylum–migration nexus, blurred the distinction between asylum seekers and migrants and led governments to further restrict immigration and to employ additional tactics to curb asylum claims. Western governments adopted a series of migration control measures to deter new arrivals, by increasing pre-arrival screening, routinely detaining asylum seekers, and deporting refugees to so-called safe third countries.[31]

In order to control the spontaneous arrival of asylum seekers on their territories, Western governments also introduced a number of measures and programs aimed at processing asylum claims in regions of refugee origin. Australia was one of the first governments to introduce regional processing and soon became a model for other asylum-receiving countries. In late 2001, Canberra introduced its "Pacific Solution" to deal with increasing numbers of boat arrivals on Australian shores from Indonesia carrying asylum seekers originating from South Asia and the Middle East.[32] Australian policy entailed off-shore interception of boat loads of refugees, transfer of these refugees to neighboring islands for processing, and mandatory detention of all land arrivals of asylum seekers. Several European governments tried to adopt similar programs and proposed initiatives which included the return of asylum seekers to regions of origin outside the European Union, the establishment of regional refugee-processing centers, and processing of asylum applications beyond Europe's frontiers.

Several refugee-hosting states expressed their concern about these new approaches, as illustrated by their participation at an inter-governmental meeting in Geneva on 7 March 2003.[33] Most refugee-hosting states noted that it would be unreasonable to expect a host state in a region of conflict—a Turkey, an Iran, a Pakistan, a Kenya, or a Thailand—to agree to the return of asylum seekers from European countries to their territories when they are already hosting large numbers of refugees. Iran, burdened with millions of Afghan refugees for over two decades, called for "fair burden- and responsibility-sharing" and doubted the applicability of local integration in massive and protracted refugee populations. Turkey spoke out against regional agreements and Pakistan noted that host countries are increasingly left with sole responsibility for refugees because of dwindling international support and interest. Thailand expressed concern that regional processing would become a mechanism of "burden shifting," not burden sharing.

More generally, efforts by Western states to contain refugees in their regions of origin, coupled with a rise in external pressures on states in the developing world, placed significant strain on asylum countries in the South, especially in Africa and Asia. In response, states in the South placed additional restrictions on asylum. Some states limited the quantity of asylum they offered to refugees, by closing their borders to prevent arrivals, by pushing for the early and often unsustainable return of refugees to their country of origin, and, in exceptional cases, forcibly expelling entire refugee populations. More generally, states placed limits on the quality of asylum they offered to refugees, by denying them the social and economic rights contained in the 1951 Convention, such as freedom of movement and the right to seek employment. Many states in the developing world insisted that refugees remain in isolated and insecure refugee camps, cut off from the local community, and fully dependent on dwindling international assistance. States justified these restrictions by emphasizing the fact that the poorest states in the international system host more than 80 percent of the world's refugees, that the mass influx and prolonged presence of these refugees had a negative impact on the host country and host community, that the international donor community had become increasingly reluctant to provide the financial support required to host these refugees, and that the presence of these refugees posed a number of security concerns.

Global Consultations and Convention Plus initiatives

In response to the decline in asylum in both the North and the South, the growing disillusionment of states with the 1951 Convention and the emergence of clear gaps in the protection framework, UNHCR launched a major initiative in late 2000 to seek a convergence between the protection needs of refugees and the interests of states. This process, called the Global Consultations on International Protection, brought together Northern and Southern states, NGOs, recognized experts in refugee law and UNHCR to "shore up support for the international framework of protection, and to explore the scope for enhancing protection through new approaches, which nevertheless respect the concerns and constraints of states and other actors."[34] Lasting nearly two years, the Global Consultations process considered the broad range of concerns expressed by Northern and Southern states in the previous decade, including issues not specifically addressed by the 1951 Convention.

There were two major outcomes from the Global Consultations process. The first was a Declaration adopted by more than 100 states in December 2001 at a meeting in Geneva to mark the 50th anniversary of the 1951 Convention. The Declaration reaffirmed the importance of the 1951 Convention as the cornerstone of international refugee protection, and reaffirmed "the fundamental importance of UNHCR as the multilateral institution with the mandate to provide international protection to refugees and to promote durable solutions."[35] The most significant outcome of the process, however, was the Agenda for Protection, endorsed by the General Assembly in 2002.[36] The Agenda for Protection outlines a series of activities and priorities that were intended to meet the concerns of states and strengthen the international protection of refugees and asylum seekers. Structured around five goals, the Agenda for Protection calls for specific action by UNHCR, states and NGOs to enhance respect for the principles of the 1951 Convention, respond to the security implications of refugee movements, enhance burden sharing with countries of first asylum, make durable solutions more predictable, and address the specific protection needs of refugee women and children.[37]

While comprehensive in scope, the Agenda for Protection has been limited in its impact in the years following its adoption. This may be for several reasons. First, the Agenda may have been too broad, addressing a vast range of issues without focusing on individual issues in depth. The Agenda was also not a binding agreement, and consequently suffers from the same limitations as other non-binding international agreements. Finally, the Agenda did not benefit from universal support within UNHCR. The Global Consultations process was widely seen within the organization as an initiative led by the protection sections of UNHCR and a final inheritance from the time of Sadako Ogata. In fact, elements of UNHCR began to distance themselves from the Agenda before it was formally completed. Shortly after assuming office in 2001, Ruud Lubbers announced a new set of initiatives that would begin before the Global Consultations ended, as outlined below. This created significant confusion within UNHCR and frustration on the part of the donor community, who had provided significant financial support to the Global Consultations process. As a result, the status of the Agenda for Protection within the international refugee protection regime remains uncertain, and its potential largely unrealized.

The initiatives launched by Lubbers shortly after taking office, collectively referred to as "Convention Plus," were motivated largely by the High Commissioner's desire to re-engage the interests of European donor states. Convention Plus attempted to develop new inter-state agreements to supplement the 1951 Convention and to enhance the prospects of solutions for refugees in regions of origin. The initiatives aimed to increase burden sharing by increasing the level of donor commitment to host countries in regions of origin and by channeling this new, abstract commitment into finding durable solutions to specific protracted refugee situations. These aims were to be achieved both through general inter-state agreements and more focused Comprehensive Plans of Action, based on the precedents of the Indochinese CPA and CIREFCA. Reflecting this framework, Convention Plus divided into two main areas: the generic work and the situation-specific work.

Within the context of the generic work, UNHCR sought to forge new agreements on resettlement, irregular secondary movements (ISM), and targeted development assistance (TDA) to improve access to durable solutions and protection capacities in regions of origin. The resettlement strand attempted to reach an understanding of the important role that resettlement can play alongside other durable solutions for refugees.[38] The irregular migration debate attempted to define the circumstances in which a state may return a refugee to a first country of asylum[39] through which that individual has already found international protection. The development debate focused on the way in which development assistance could be used to promote repatriation, local integration or self-sufficiency for refugees in developing countries.[40] A common feature of these three areas was their attempt to determine states' responsibilities for refugee protection and the provision of durable solutions, and sought to address Northern states' concerns with the irregular movement of asylum seekers, and Southern states' concerns with protracted refugee situations and the absence of international burden sharing. To facilitate these discussions, UNHCR initiated the so-called High Commissioner's Forum—a series of multilateral meetings in Geneva between states and UNHCR that were separate from the usual cycle of UNHCR Executive Committee meetings.

The Convention Plus process largely failed to meet its initial aims by the time it ended in November 2005 and the intended new agreements were never reached. The only output that came close to meeting this status was the Multilateral Framework of Understandings on Resettlement, yet even this was a modest and uncontroversial statement that entailed no binding commitments and was only intended to apply in conjunction with the agreements on the other strands, rendering its ultimate relevance extremely limited.[41] The failure of Convention Plus was largely due to the polarization of positions between Northern and Southern states in discussions on development and migration. In the development debates, Southern states were left disillusioned by both the reluctance of donor states to offer significant additional assistance and the exclusion of host states from many of the "donor-only" discussions. Meanwhile, Northern states were left disillusioned by the apparent unwillingness of Southern host states to countenance local integration or self-sufficiency opportunities for refugees on their territories. In the irregular migration debate, Northern states wanted a definition of "effective protection" that would make return and readmission of refugees to regions of origin easier. For their part, Southern states wanted a definition that would ensure a greater financial commitment by donors to strengthen the refugee protection capacity of host states without this being related to readmission. For its part, UNHCR was unable to overcome this North–South impasse, a factor which contributed significantly to the overall failure of the Convention Plus process.

Under the banner of Convention Plus, UNHCR also attempted to formulate Comprehensive Plans of Action to resolve a number of longstanding refugee situations. The pilot case chosen was the situation of Somali refugees, and UNHCR worked on developing a CPA for Somali refugees between 2004 and 2005. The project focused on trying to build protection capacity and enhance access to durable solutions for Somali refugees in Djibouti, Ethiopia, Kenya, and the Yemen, and IDPs and returnees in Somaliland and Central and Southern Somalia. The focus on Somalia was chosen largely because the project's key donors—the European Commission, Denmark, the Netherlands, and the UK—were particularly concerned about the large number of Somali asylum seekers and refugees moving onwards to Europe. UNHCR hoped that this political interest, motivated primarily by concerns with migration and security, might lead to a commitment to protection and durable solutions in the region of origin. In the end, however, there was little donor interest in the plan formulated by UNHCR, and the Somali CPA was never launched.

Although the Somalia CPA purported to draw upon the highly successful precedents of the Indochinese CPA and CIREFCA, it had many differences that highlighted the reasons for its failure. First, the project's failure can be partly linked to the problematic choice to focus on Somalia—a state in which ongoing conflict limited the scope for repatriation and in which the absence of a viable government in Somalia precluded the meaningful participation of the country of origin, a key factor for success in both the Indochinese CPA and CIREFCA. Second, unlike the two historical precedents, the Somali CPA was not based on a sustained political process, but was conceived by the Africa Bureau as a technocratic exercise that, like ICARA I and II, would culminate in a one-off pledging conference. With no inter-state dialogue along North–South lines, there was little opportunity to build donor and host state confidence in the viability of the project. Third, unlike in the two previous CPAs, UNHCR failed to commit high level, politically talented staff to working on the project, and it received low priority within UNHCR. Finally, the Somalia CPA did not adequately link humanitarian factors with the underlying and crucially important economic, political and security factors. The principal weakness of the Somalia CPA is that it remained divorced from the political efforts to re-establish a central government in Mogadishu.[42] The failure of the Somali CPA should therefore not be seen as illustrative of the limitations of a CPA-like approach, but as a process that highlights the need for UNHCR to learn the lessons of history and better appreciate the conditions under which its previous CPAs were successful.

In addition to these Convention Plus projects, a number of other initiatives were launched within UNHCR during the Lubbers era, some of which proved to be more successful. UNHCR created an Afghanistan Comprehensive Solutions Unit, which worked systematically with political actors to pursue durable solutions and enhanced refugee protection for the more than 2 million Afghan refugees in Pakistan and Iran. Although practical progress was relatively slow, the Unit's work contributed to facilitating more sustainable repatriation and engaging with host governments to take account of the complex migratory networks that are intertwined with the situation of Afghan refugees. This initiative was pioneering for UNHCR in the sense that it allowed two high-level members of staff to work full-time on a specific protracted refugee situation, primarily through working with political actors in the host states and country of origin. The Lubbers era also witnessed the revival of the use of self-sufficiency as an alternative method of protection, pending access to durable solutions. Through promoting examples of UNHCR-supported self-reliance projects for refugees in Uganda and Zambia, the Office attempted to persuade other states to countenance providing refugees with greater freedom of movement and access to livelihood and employment opportunities. Most Southern states, however, continued to be highly sceptical about allowing self-sufficiency projects, seeing them as a backdoor effort to locally integrate refugees.

When evaluating the Lubbers era, a number of limitations in the work of UNHCR clearly emerge. In particular, UNHCR was often far too closely aligned with the interests of a small number of European donor states during Lubbers' term, often alienating Southern states. For example, Convention Plus emerged with very minimal consultation, and was viewed by many Southern states with suspicion. During the Convention Plus period, UNHCR was frequently seen to be compromising its core mandate in order to integrate the emerging migration control debate and adapt to the so-called asylum–migration nexus. Moreover, much of Lubbers' term was characterized by a lack of clear and coherent strategy, with initiatives emerging in an often *ad hoc* manner.

Notwithstanding these limitations, Lubbers' term also had a number of strengths. Its focus on the need to develop a stronger framework for burden sharing and for developing comprehensive approaches to overcoming protracted refugee situations was significant. Furthermore, a range of innovative ideas emerged during the term, particularly from the Convention Plus experience. For example, the work of Convention Plus highlights the important potential role that could be played by a small, permanent and politically-oriented secretariat within the Office. Meanwhile, the High Commissioner's Forum offered a highly innovative site for multilateral dialogue and debate on the development of new normative commitments. The Lubbers era also saw the revival of the notion of refugee aid and development, and the recognition of the potentially important role of development actors such as UNDP and the World Bank in enhancing refugee protection and access to durable solutions.

Guterres and the changing international humanitarian environment

Lubbers resigned as High Commissioner in February 2005 following allegations of sexual harassment.[43] Amid high hopes of addressing divisions left within the organization, António Guterres took office as the new High Commissioner for Refugees in mid-June 2005. He was immediately confronted with the challenge of responding to additional changes in the nature of forced displacement. By 2005, the restrictive asylum policies of Northern states had contributed to a significant reduction in the number of asylum seekers in industrialized countries, with European states alone receiving some 36 percent fewer asylum claims in 2004 than it had in 2001.[44] At the same time, however, the number of IDPs remained at about 25 million worldwide and took on growing international significance. During these years, extraordinary natural disasters, such as the Indian Ocean tsunami of December 2004 and the Pakistan earthquake of October 2005, also generated massive numbers of displaced people attracting widespread media attention. These developments led UNHCR to become increasingly involved, not only in IDP operations but also in international responses to those displaced by natural disasters, representing another significant expansion of UNHCR's understanding of its mandate.

Guterres undertook a number of initiatives in response to this changing international humanitarian environment and the shift in the dynamics of forced displacement. In particular, UNHCR became increasingly involved in IDP issues. During the late 1990s and early twenty-first century, the discussion on new international norms surrounding the "responsibility to protect,"[45] coupled with renewed efforts at UN reform to coordinate international responses to IDP situations, led to calls for UNHCR to take a greater role in responding to the protection and assistance needs of IDPs. This was formalized in September 2005, when IASC assigned UNHCR the lead role for protection, shelter and camp management in IDP situations. As discussed in Chapter 5, this new responsibility dominated the agenda of UNHCR's senior managers in Geneva and staff in the field, and had significant implications for the Office's traditional work. During 2006–2007, Guterres tasked the Office's senior managers in Headquarters and the field to formulate plans and undertake activities to ensure that UNHCR fulfilled its leadership role in existing and emerging IDP situations. A huge amount of time and energy went into strengthening capacity and preparedness within the organization, creating stand-by arrangements with NGOs, training staff in protection and international legal standards and building stockpiles of supplies for new humanitarian emergencies.

In mid-2007, UNHCR was conducting a wide range of protection and assistance activities for IDPs in 24 countries with approximately 18 million IDPs.[46] If the new international coordination arrangements for IDPs and victims of natural disasters do result in a more effective pooling and deployment of resources, it is likely that UNHCR's involvement with non-refugee emergencies will continue to grow, representing one of the most significant evolutions in the interpretation of UNHCR's mandate.

It remains questionable whether the new UN collaborative approach and the role of UNHCR will be effective. As argued elsewhere in this book, UNHCR has extensive experience in dealing with refugee emergencies and with refugee protection but only limited experience with operating in conditions involving internal displacement. Given that the number of IDPs is far greater than the number of refugees, the Office needs to significantly retool and upgrade its emergency capacity and protection functions to meet the additional caseload. The fulfillment of these new tasks within the UN collaborative approach depends on considerable extra funding and strong and sustained political support, neither of which is guaranteed.

A second preoccupation under Guterres has been the fundamental reconsideration of UNHCR's management structures and spending priorities. In early 2006, Guterres launched a major management reform process with the mandate to reconsider a wide range of structural, staffing, and procedural issues. The exercise was primarily initiated in response to donor pressure to reduce the size and budget of UNHCR's Geneva headquarters, and to redeploy these resources to UNHCR's field operations. A second motivation was a desire to make UNHCR more effective and responsive, especially in light of changes in the nature of displacement and other reforms taking place within the UN system. While the results of this process are pending, early decisions relating to the outposting of administrative and operational support functions outside Geneva, the redeployment of a number of functions to regional centers, and the eventual downsizing of headquarters by some 20 percent indicate that this process will have a significant impact on the work of UNHCR.

In addition to these policy and management concerns, the Office faced a number of challenges to its operational capacity in the first two years of Guterres' term, including displacement along the Chad/Darfur border and in and around Iraq. Following the eruption of violence in Sudan's western Darfur region in early 2003, some 1.6 million persons were internally displaced and over 200,000 refugees fled across the border into neighboring Chad. Responding to the needs of these populations has posed significant challenges to UNHCR. Logistically, the displaced populations are spread across a vast and inaccessible area. Security of both displaced persons and humanitarian workers has also been a significant concern, as armed elements from both sides of the conflict have attacked refugee and IDP camps. Likewise, violence in Central and Southern Iraq forcibly displaced millions of Iraqis in the years following the 2003 invasion. In mid-2007, UNHCR estimated that 2.2 million Iraqis had taken refuge in neighboring countries, primarily Syria and Jordan, and some 2 million were internally displaced. Overwhelmed by the needs of the displaced, and in response to appeals for assistance from host states in the region, UNHCR convened an international conference in Geneva in April 2007. The major objectives were to draw attention to the much neglected humanitarian consequences of the conflict and to rally donor support for its activities in the region. In July 2007, UNHCR increased its budget for displaced Iraqis to US$123 million, and expressed dismay at the continued reluctance of donor countries to fulfill pledges made at the April conference. Continued upheaval in Iraq and Darfur, combined with limited international commitment to stem the violence and address the humanitarian consequences of the conflicts, suggest that managing these two crises will be a prolonged challenge for UNHCR.

At the same time, UNHCR has committed considerable resources to managing massive repatriation operations in Afghanistan, South Sudan, West Africa, and Central Africa. Following the peace accord between the Sudanese government and the Sudanese People's Liberation Army/Movement in January 2005, UNHCR launched a repatriation program in December 2005 for the hundreds of thousands of South Sudanese refugees in six neighboring host countries. Repatriation efforts, however, have been frustrated by the devastation caused by decades of war and the desperate lack of infrastructure needed to sustain the repatriation and reintegration of such a large population. Similar concerns, coupled with continued insecurity, have frustrated efforts to repatriate Afghan refugees from Pakistan and Iran following the successful completion of the Bonn process in December 2001. While some 4 million Afghans are reported to have repatriated since 2002, localized conflict and endemic poverty continue to frustrate reintegration efforts for these refugees and prospects of repatriation for the estimated 3.5 million refugees who remain in exile.

At the end of 2006, these challenges of repatriation, coupled with the rise in new refugee crises in Iraq and Chad, resulted in the first increase in global refugee numbers for five years. As of 31 December

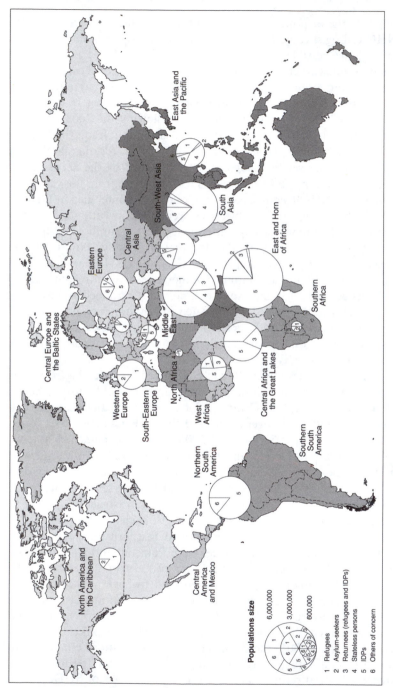

Figure 3.1 Populations of concern to UNHCR as of 1 January 2007.

2006, UNHCR reported that there were 9.9 million refugees in the world, and that the total population of concern to the Office was 32.9 million. Figure 3.1 illustrates the extent of UNHCR's global responsibilities at the start of 2007.

Underlying these numbers is the increasingly protracted nature of most refugee situations. During the 1990s, most refugees were in emergency situations, and the focus of the international community was to provide life-saving assistance and shelter in refugee camps. More than two-thirds of refugees in the world at the end of 2006, however, were in protracted refugee situations, having been in exile for more than five years, often contained in isolated and insecure camps. Refugee situations are also lasting longer as international responses to failed and fragile states prove inadequate. In fact, the average duration of a refugee situation rose from 9 years in 1993 to 17 years in 2004.[47] The plight of these refugees has recently risen on the international agenda, as some states, NGOs, researchers and UNHCR have drawn attention to the rising challenge of finding solutions to these protracted refugee situations.[48] As discussed in Chapter 5, however, finding solutions to these situations remains a major challenge for UNHCR.

Conclusion

Over the past five and a half decades, the nature and scope of UNHCR's work have changed considerably in response to the changing nature of forced displacement. From a small Office of some 30 staff based mostly in Europe in the early 1950s, UNHCR is now a global organization with a staff of more than 6,500 in 116 countries. UNHCR now works not only with refugees, but also with IDPs, returnees, stateless and a number of other "persons of concern." With an increase in the number of persons displaced by natural disasters and a dramatic rise in the number of economic migrants in the world more generally, coupled with predictions that these numbers will rise further with global warming and globalization, the challenge of forced migration is likely to increase in scale and complexity in the future.

Given these prospects, UNHCR will likely be called upon to assume ever greater responsibilities in increasingly complex situations in the future. As the Office faces these challenges, however, it is essential to consider the relevance of UNHCR's core mandate responsibilities of ensuring international protection for refugees and finding a durable solution to their plight. Many scholars have insisted in recent years that UNHCR is unique among global institutions as the only organization with a specific mandate to ensure the protection of refugees and to find solutions to their plight. They believe that UNHCR should therefore fulfill these core mandate responsibilities before assuming additional functions, including a role in responding to IDP situations, development initiatives or work in countries of origin.[49] The next two chapters examine the debates surrounding these issues, and the pressures placed on UNHCR's mandate by the changing nature of forced migration.

4   UNHCR as a global institution

Structures, relationships and the politics of funding

UNHCR is the only global organization with a specific mandate to ensure the protection of refugees and to find solutions to their plight. It is, however, unable to pursue its mandate independently. Instead, UNHCR is structurally and operationally linked to a wide range of other actors in the international system, including donor and refugee-hosting states, other UN agencies, international, national and local NGOs, and a number of other actors. UNHCR is also dependent on voluntary contributions from donors to carry out its work, and the interest and priorities of donor states have consequently played a significant role in the work and evolution of the organization. In this way, UNHCR is both an independent actor in the international system with a specific mandate and an organization that is deeply enmeshed in a diverse and changing set of relationships with a growing number of other actors. While each of these actors has their own interests and priorities, UNHCR is increasingly reliant upon them for the exercise of its core mandate responsibilities.

UNHCR has worked with donor and host states, other UN agencies and NGOs since its inception. The Office's relationships with these actors have, however, changed significantly over time, both in response to the changing nature of displacement and in response to UNHCR's evolving interpretation of its mandate. The most important of these relationships remains the Office's relationship with donors, who control the evolution and direction of UNHCR's work through the tight control of the organization's resources.

At the same time, UNHCR has increasingly become a complex international organization with a truly global presence. In a wide range of operational contexts, the Office must respond to local political realities, dynamics and interests as it seeks to advance its mandate. The result is not only a significant diversification of working environments for UNHCR—in environments ranging from the Chad/

Sudan border to the corridors of European bureaucracy in Brussels—
but also a complex web of relationships between the organization and
a diverse array of external actors. Ensuring the health of these relationships has been a central challenge to UNHCR since its creation,
and will remain so in the future. Understanding the nature of these
relationships is consequently an increasingly important aspect of
understanding the organization's work in a changing international
system.

UNHCR is also distinctive among UN agencies. It is both an individual, represented in the High Commissioner, and a bureaucracy,
with its own unique culture and value system. The High Commissioner has little or no political authority, but is vested with considerable moral authority and legitimacy, dating back not just to the
Office's founding in 1950, but also to the time of Fridtjof Nansen and
the League of Nations. UNHCR is also an organization with its own
identity, comprising some 6,500 individuals of different nationalities
who share similar values. As the organization has grown and as its
interpretation of its mandate has expanded, however, the identity of
the organization has come under increasing pressure. If UNHCR, as
both the High Commissioner and the organization, is to continue to
exert its moral authority and leadership in the international system,
these pressures and tensions need to be resolved.

Finally, one cannot fully understand UNHCR without a knowledge
of its organizational culture. There exists no other UN agency where
values and principled ideas are so central to the mandate and *raison
d'être* of the institution, or where some committed staff members are
willing to place their lives in danger to defend the proposition that
persecuted individuals need protection. It is, however, important to
not simply take this rhetoric at face value. As outlined in previous
chapters, UNHCR has had both many success and many failures
during its history. There remains, however, very little external scrutiny
of UNHCR and no formal mechanism through which the Office is
held accountable for its actions. The Office must be held accountable
for operational failures and shortcomings and when it abuses its position or does not live up to its principles. More significantly, the Office
must be accountable for those instances where its actions threaten,
rather than enhance, the protection of refugees. In describing the
structures and dynamics behind UNHCR's work, this chapter highlights the on-going importance of transparency, cooperation, leadership and accountability. It explains UNHCR's position within the
wider UN system, the role of its Executive Committee, its internal
structures, and external relationships.

UNHCR within the UN system

As outlined in Chapter 1, UNHCR was created by the General Assembly in December 1950. The General Assembly resolution that established the Office detailed the place of the new organization within the UN system. The first paragraph of the Statute of the Office of the United Nations High Commissioner for Refugees states that the High Commissioner was to act "under the authority of the General Assembly" and was to pursue its mandate "under the auspices of the United Nations."[1] The Statute goes on to specify that the High Commissioner for Refugees shall report annually to the General Assembly through ECOSOC on the Office's activities and that UNHCR shall follow policy directives issued by General Assembly or ECOSOC.

UNHCR's Statute also gave the General Assembly the authority to determine the continued existence of UNHCR after an initial three-year mandate. For more than 50 years, UNHCR was only given limited extensions on its mandate by the General Assembly. In successive annual resolutions, the General Assembly recognized the on-going importance of the work of UNHCR, but continued to return only a limited extension on the mandate of the organization, usually for an additional five years. Many observers of UNHCR believed that the resulting uncertainty limited UNHCR's ability to engage in a number of longer-term activities, especially in areas relating to development programs in host countries and countries of refugee origin. Addressing this limitation was therefore one of the priorities of High Commissioner Lubbers. In December 2003, the General Assembly passed a resolution that finally removed the temporal limitation on the continuation of UNHCR and confirmed the Office as a program of the United Nations "until the refugee problem is solved."[2]

More generally, the authority of the General Assembly to issue policy directives to UNHCR has played a crucial role in the expansion of the Office's mandate since its inception. While initially given a limited mandate, UNHCR turned repeatedly throughout the Cold War to the General Assembly to authorize the Office's involvement in emerging refugee situations in Africa and Asia, as outlined in Chapter 2. During this period, the General Assembly also played a significant role by authorizing special resolutions in response to particular refugee situations. For example, major multilateral efforts to address refugee situation in Africa through the ICARA process and in Indochina through the CPA were underpinned by General Assembly resolutions. Since the end of the Cold War, however, the continued expansion of

UNHCR's area of work has increasingly been at the request of the UN Secretary-General and the Security Council, as outlined in Chapter 3.

Notwithstanding this increased involvement of the Secretary-General and the Security Council, there is a widespread perception within the UN system that refugees are UNHCR's "problem." This perception, likely a result of the territoriality and competition between UN agencies that dominated the 1990s, has frustrated efforts to articulate a more comprehensive and holistic engagement in issues relating to refugees. As outlined in Chapters 2 and 3, however, solutions to refugee situations have been more successful when they include the sustained engagement of a wide range of actors within the UN system, especially security and development actors, such as DPKO and UNDP. In the context of wider discussions about system-wide coherence and the ability of the UN system to work in a more effective, collaborative and coherent way in response to humanitarian challenges, the needs of refugees should not be overlooked.

The creation of the UN Peacebuilding Commission in 2005, for example, offers an opportunity for more collective action by a broader range of UN actors to find solutions for refugees. With its focus on post-conflict recovery, the Commission could play an important role in drawing together the necessary range of actors to address both the underlying causes of displacement and the preconditions for sustainable repatriation. At the same time, UNHCR should ensure that the Commission does not overlook the links between refugees and the regional dynamics of peacebuilding, especially given the potentially destabilizing role that early and unsustainable repatriation, along with the presence of armed elements in neighboring host states, can play during post-conflict reconstruction.[3]

UNHCR's Executive Committee

Another significant role played by the General Assembly and ECOSOC is in determining the size and membership of the Executive Committee of the Program of the United Nations High Commissioner for Refugees (ExCom).[4] Established by the General Assembly in 1958, ExCom was initially to consist of 20–25 UN Member States, selected by ECOSOC "on the widest possible geographic basis from those States with a demonstrated interest in, and devotion to, the solution of the refugee problem."[5] While retaining authority over the work of UNHCR, the General Assembly mandated ExCom to perform a number of executive and advisory functions.

ExCom continues to perform many of these functions. During its annual plenary session in Geneva, typically lasting one week and held in early October, ExCom is responsible for approving UNHCR's budget and program for the following year, for reaching conclusions on international refugee protection policy issues, and for providing guidance on UNHCR's management, objectives, and priorities. As a subsidiary organ of the General Assembly, ExCom members also submit an annual report for the consideration and endorsement of the Third Committee of the General Assembly. In addition to its annual meeting, the ExCom Standing Committee meets several times each year to further the work of ExCom, largely in areas relating to management, finances, and operational issues.

As of April 2007, ExCom consisted of 72 Member States (Table 4.1).[6] This represents a significant growth in the number of ExCom members during its 50-year existence. From 25 ExCom members at its first meeting, the number rose slowly in response to the increased membership of the United Nations, to 43 members in 1988. With the end of the Cold War, however, the number has grown significantly, with the membership rising to 50 in 1995, up to 72 members in 2007. Almost 30 states have joined ExCom since the end of the Cold War. As a result of this rapid expansion, ExCom has become a large and cumbersome body. Not only are there too many participants, but the issues are complex and numerous, and meetings are not really a forum for organizational guidance. Individual donor governments and some key host states, not ExCom, have come to establish the priorities that guide UNHCR's program direction.

The composition of ExCom has meant that many of the broad contours of international politics are reflected in ExCom deliberations. Specifically, observers of ExCom have noticed an increasing divide between industrialized states, who are traditionally the largest donors to UNHCR's program, and developing countries, who host the overwhelming majority of the world's refugees. The divergent perspectives of these two groups of states have been clearly evident for more than a decade during ExCom meetings. In an effort to overcome this North–South divide, ExCom has adopted the practice of a rotating Chairmanship between Northern and Southern states. While this is an important step towards addressing some of the tensions that underlie ExCom meetings, more progress is clearly required. North–South divisions have significantly limited the work of ExCom in recent years to adopt conclusions that could enhance protection and ensure solutions for refugees, especially through agreement on areas such local integration and burden sharing.

Table 4.1 ExCom members as of April 2007

Algeria	Argentina	Australia
Austria	Bangladesh	Belgium
Brazil	Canada	Chile
China	Colombia	Costa Rica
Côte d'Ivoire	Cyprus	Democratic Republic
Denmark	Ecuador	of the Congo
Egypt	Estonia	Ethiopia
Finland	France	Germany
Ghana	Greece	Guinea
Holy See	Hungary	India
Iran (Islamic Republic of)	Ireland	Israel
Italy	Japan	Jordan
Kenya	Lebanon	Lesotho
Madagascar	Mexico	Morocco
Mozambique	Namibia	The Netherlands
New Zealand	Nicaragua	Nigeria
Norway	Pakistan	The Philippines
Poland	Portugal	Republic of Korea
Romania	Russian Federation	Serbia
Somalia	South Africa	Spain
Sudan	Sweden	Switzerland
Thailand	Tunisia	Turkey
Uganda	United Kingdom	United Republic
United States of America	Venezuela (Bolivarian	of Tanzania
Zambia	Republic of)	Yemen

Source: UNHCR Global Report (2006).

There have also been concerns in recent years about the domestic refugee policies of a number of ExCom members. While member states are expected to have a "demonstrated interest in, and devotion to, the solution of the refugee problem,"[7] critics have argued that the actions of certain members represent some of the more significant breaches of international refugee protection standards. One refugee rights monitoring group found that longstanding member states such as Tanzania and the US had engaged in *refoulement*, while member states such as Algeria, Bangladesh and Kenya placed severe limitations on the freedom of movement and right to seek employment of refugees on their territory, notwithstanding the fact that they were all signatories of the major international refugee instruments which prohibit such acts.[8] Current ExCom membership also includes countries like Bangladesh and Thailand, who have signed neither the 1951 Convention nor the 1967 Protocol but who have hosted significant refugee populations for decades.

Such factors point to a need to re-examine the composition and role of ExCom in light of its original mandate, especially given the role that ExCom could play in providing the formal accountability mechanism that UNHCR so desperately needs. To better serve this function, ExCom member states and UNHCR need to streamline the agency's governance arrangements by making ExCom a more assertive advisory body with serious oversight functions and a capacity for organizational guidance. As states scrutinize UNHCR, they need also to become more self-critical in their own roles in refugee protection and assistance. ExCom should reaffirm the core principles of refugee protection through the work of its Standing Committees, and member states should not undermine UNHCR by adopting policies that violate international refugee norms and set undesirable precedents for refugee protection elsewhere. These issues reinforce the potentially significant role that an independent monitoring mechanism could provide in the oversight of both UNHCR's programs and state activities in refugee protection and assistance.

UNHCR's internal structure and dynamics

It would be problematic to speak of UNHCR exclusively as a single coherent actor without recognizing the complexity of relationships within the organization. UNHCR exists not only in its Geneva headquarters, but also in over 100 countries in a wide range of circumstances and organizational arrangements. A vast web of relationships in a range of geographic and political contexts is therefore the reality of UNHCR, with significant implications for the ability of the organization to fulfill its mandate. To understand the issues at the core of UNHCR's internal structure and dynamics, it is important to begin by understanding how the organization has grown over the past 50 years. When UNHCR began operations on 1 January 1951, it had a staff of 34, based primarily in Geneva, and a budget of only US$300,000. In fact, the staff of UNHCR was so small at the beginning that the entire staff gathered around a single piano at the Office's 1951 staff Christmas party to sing carols, while the High Commissioner himself played the piano. More than 50 years later, UNHCR has a staff of more than 6,500 in more than 116 countries with an annual budget of over US$1 billion.

Headquarters

Roughly a third of UNHCR's staff is located in UNHCR's head-quarters in Geneva. Headquarters is, in turn, divided into a number of departments and divisions (Figure 4.1). At the organizational top of headquarters, and also on the top floor of UNHCR's seven-story building, is the Executive Office, including the High Commissioner, the Deputy High Commissioner, the Assistant High Commissioner for Protection, the Assistant High Commissioner for Operations, and a range of other executive officers. The Department of International Protection is under the responsibility of the Assistant High Commissioner for Protection. The Division of Operational Services and the five Regional Bureaus are under the responsibility of the Assistant High Commissioner for Operations. Finally, a range of management and administrative functions—including the Division of External Relations, the Division of Human Resources Management and the Division of Financial and Supply Management—are under the responsibility of the Deputy High Commissioner.

As outlined in Chapters 2 and 3, a recurring source of tension within UNHCR since the mid-1960s has been between sections of head-quarters responsible for protection and those responsible for operations. Prior to the mid-1980s, the protection branch of headquarters was above operations within the hierarchy of the organization, reflecting for many the emphasis on UNHCR's core mandate responsibilities of protection and solutions. In an effort to make UNHCR more operational, and therefore responsive to donors, High Commissioner Hocké effectively demoted protection within the organization in the mid-1980s, making the Head of Protection equal in seniority to the Directors of the individual Regional Bureaus. It was not until 2006 that the post of Assistant High Commissioner for Protection was created in an effort to give additional prominence to UNHCR's protection functions within the politics of headquarters.

The downgrading of protection had significant implications for UNHCR policy and practice during the 1990s, especially when the operational priorities of the regional Bureaus came into conflict with the priorities of the protection section of UNHCR. This tension came to the fore in December 1996, when UNHCR was confronted with Tanzania's expulsion of all Rwandan refugees from its territory. The Division of International Protection argued that UNHCR should criticize Tanzania, and denounce the forced return of Rwandans as *refoulement*. In contrast, the Africa Bureau believed that such a stance was not pragmatic, as it would hinder UNHCR's position to assist

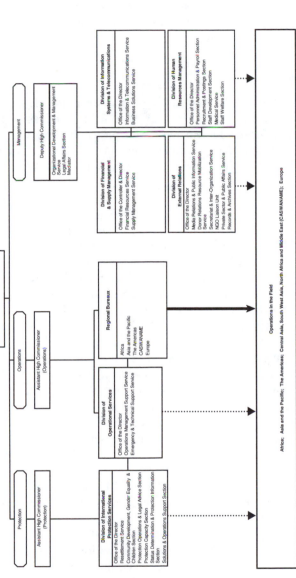

Figure 4.1 Organization of UNHCR headquarters as of 1 July 2006.
Source: UNHCR Global Report (2006).

those who were being forcibly returned. In the end, High Commissioner Ogata accepted the advice of the Africa Bureau, effectively condoning the forced repatriation of hundreds of thousands of refugees.[9] Resolving such tensions between protection and operations remains a key challenge for UNHCR.

The field

The majority of UNHCR staff members work outside of headquarters, in what is collectively known as "the field." Offices in the field are responsible for the implementation of protection and assistance policies and strategies in the area under their jurisdiction. These areas may be in countries of refugee origin, in host countries in regions of refugee origin, or in asylum and donor countries, in industrialized states or in developing countries. In each of these locations, UNHCR staff must interact with an array of actors, interests and politics as diverse and complex at those at the international level in Geneva. These tasks are varied. They must negotiate access with national governments, implement programs with an array of partners, and endeavor to implement global policy in a local reality. In each of these situations, UNHCR staff must negotiate with government counterparts, NGOs, regional organizations, diplomatic missions, other UN agencies, civil society and refugees themselves to further UNHCR's core mandate and other activities.

In many instances, UNHCR has to engage with governments that are uncooperative, troublesome and even hostile to UNHCR. Given that the Office can only work in a country if it is invited to do so by the government, it ignores the importance of local politics at its peril. Governments have a range of mechanism for frustrating the work of UNHCR, including preventing access to regions of the country, isolating UNHCR Representatives and denying entry for visiting missions from headquarters. An extreme consequence of ignoring these dynamics is the real danger of UNHCR being expelled from a country.

The management structure of UNHCR's presence in a given country differs in response to the operational reality and local conditions there.[10] In some instances, a number of countries are covered by a single UNHCR Regional Office. In countries with larger populations of concern to UNHCR, and where the organization has been granted access, the Office will typically seek the government's permission to establish a country office, headed by a UNHCR Representative. In countries with large and geographically dispersed populations of concern to UNHCR, and in instances where the population of concern is located at some distance from the capital city, UNHCR will seek to establish additional sub-offices and field offices. A sub-office is usually established in a strategic regional location in which local government officials with authority over the refugee-populated area are based. A field office is also a full UNHCR office, but typically located in a more remote part of the country, and is usually administered by a sub-office or a country office.

UNHCR field offices are linked to headquarters in a number of ways. Every field office must draft a Country Operations Plan for submission to their respective Regional Bureau in headquarters every year. In addition, as UNHCR programs have become more complex, and as reporting requirements have multiplied, field offices are spending an increasing portion of their time writing reports and answering questions from headquarters. UNHCR staff in the field increasingly complain about the seemingly uncoordinated and multiplying demands from headquarters for written reports and the volume of policies, guidelines and directives issued from headquarters that the field is expected to rapidly implement. Many staff in the field believe that these requirements from headquarters are not only unnecessary, but take valuable time away from their protection work with refugees. Tensions between the field and headquarters increasingly foster the perception among staff in the field that headquarters is disconnected from the conditions, needs, and reality of field operations.

Organizational culture

One cannot fully understand UNHCR without understanding its organizational culture. Values and principled ideas are central to the ethos of UNHCR, and the rising instances of staff insecurity painfully illustrate that committed staff members are willing to place their lives in danger to defend the principles which the Office is mandated to uphold.[11] A review of UNHCR's organizational culture completed in 2005 found that UNHCR staff had a very strong sense of collective identity and *esprit de corps*.[12] The review found that UNHCR staff almost universally believed in the principles contained in the organization's core mandate, valued the quality of their fellow staff, and were motivated to make a positive difference to the lives of refugees. Words such as commitment, passion, love and sacrifice were used to describe the spirit of UNHCR. Even in the face of rising physical insecurity for humanitarian workers in the field, strains on family life and the stresses of working in what has sometimes been called a dysfunctional organization, UNHCR staff demonstrated an exceptional devotion to their work.

At the same time, the review concluded that the system placed too many burdens on staff. Concerns were raised about the policy of frequently rotating staff between posts, the challenges of leadership, authority and management in such a complex organization, the divisions between national and international staff within the system, the increasing tensions between headquarters and the field, and the perpetual climate of crisis within which UNHCR staff operate. The review pointed to the rising divorce rate within UNHCR—among the highest of UN agencies—the lack of long-term planning and the increasing lack of coherence within the global strategies of the organization. While UNHCR has taken some early steps to address these challenges, additional effort is required if the vibrancy of the organization is to be maintained in the years ahead.

Another significant and recurring challenge faced by UNHCR is that of structural reform and management change. Since the mid-1980s, the organization has gone through five significant downsizing and restructuring exercises. While it is too early to evaluate the most recent process, outlined in Chapter 3, previous initiatives to restructure the organization have been extremely disruptive for the Office's work, demoralizing, and ineffective. For example, restructuring efforts in the mid-1990s resulted in an exodus of highly qualified and experienced junior and middle-management staff from UNHCR, the consequences of which continue to hamper the work of the organization. Given that UNHCR's strength is widely recognized as the individuals who represent the organization around the world, such concerns cannot be taken lightly. As the early chapters of this book make clear, however, UNHCR has always been expected to exercise its mandate in an international system that is in a constant state of flux, and in cooperation with a wide range of states and UN and NGO counterparts. Change therefore is necessary if UNHCR is to remain fully effective and relevant. How to manage this change while staying true to its core mandate remains one of UNHCR's most persistent challenges.

When undertaking change within the organization, UNHCR should adopt measures to retain a greater proportion of its staff. Security needs to be improved, working conditions need to be humanized and psychological support provided where needed, particularly in difficult assignments in the field. UNHCR also should give staff more opportunities to voice their dissent and frustrations, and to offer suggestions about how to improve policies and programs. Such measures will give personnel more of a sense of working for an organization that cares about their welfare.

Finally, more can be done to increase the transparency and accountability of UNHCR, particularly regarding the decisions and programs that affect the lives of the millions of refugees and displaced people for whom it works. Improvements can be made in the organization's decision-making regarding asylum seekers' deportation, release from detention, and eligibility for resettlement to a third country or humanitarian assistance. UNHCR too infrequently has structured dialogue and communication with refugee populations or their leadership. Thus, the principal beneficiaries of UNHCR services, the refugees themselves, often have little or no means to influence or recourse in cases where the Office's programs or policies may be unsatisfactory or many even lead to harmful consequences.

UNHCR's relationships with its operational partners

From its inception, UNHCR has worked with a range of operational partners, particularly in finding solutions and providing assistance for refugees. The Office's relationship with these partners, however, has sometimes been marked by periods of competition and tension. As outlined earlier in this book, UNHCR was created with a restricted mandate and limited resources. The Office was confronted with rival international refugee organizations in the early years of its existence, thereby creating a need for UNHCR to more clearly define its role and defend its area of work in an emerging international refugee protection regime. Even after UNHCR established itself as the primary UN refugee agency, it continued to compete with other UN agencies and international and non-governmental organizations for resources and primacy within the ever expanding humanitarian community. For this reason, UNHCR's relationship with other international organizations and NGOs has been marked by both close cooperation and bitter competition.

The competition and lack of coordination, especially among UN agencies, has resulted in numerous efforts in recent years to reform the international humanitarian community. In the face of a rapid increase in humanitarian emergencies in the early 1990s, the Office of the UN Secretary General focused on strengthening the coordination of the UN's capacity to more rapidly and effectively respond to humanitarian emergencies, as outlined in Chapter 3. In March 1992, the Department of Humanitarian Affairs (DHA) was created and the UN's first Humanitarian Assistance Coordinator was appointed. At the same time, the Inter-Agency Standing Committee (IASC) was established to facilitate inter-agency coordination in humanitarian emergencies. The DHA, however, was never able to play its intended leadership role as it lacked authority, funding and support from other UN Agencies, including UNHCR. In 1997, the DHA was replaced by the Office for the Coordination of Humanitarian Affairs (OCHA) as part of a

major restructuring of the UN system under Secretary-General Kofi
Annan. As part of this restructuring process, UNHCR signed Mem-
orandums of Understanding (MoU) with its operational partners within
the UN system, clarifying areas of cooperation and the division of
responsibilities between agencies in the field.

The effectiveness of this architecture was revisited in 2005–2006 as
part of a broader effort to ensure greater coherence in the UN's response
to complex humanitarian emergencies, including IDPs and natural
disasters. The review process made a number of recommendations relating to the role of IASC at the international level and UN Resident
Coordinators and Humanitarian Coordinators in the field. The process has also resulted in the establishment of an agreed division of
labor among the UN and other international agencies, known as the
Cluster Approach. Notwithstanding these efforts, tensions remain
between UNHCR and a number of its international operational partners, both UN agencies and NGOs, on the limits of their activities and
competition over funding.

UNHCR and other international organizations

At an operational level, UNHCR works with a broad range of specialized agencies of the United Nations, international organizations,
international financial institutions, bilateral government development
partners, and regional organizations, including the African Union (AU),
the North Atlantic Treaty Organization (NATO) and the Organization
for Security and Cooperation in Europe (OSCE). Its most significant
partners, however, are the World Food Programme (WFP), UNDP,
DPKO, the International Organization for Migration (IOM) and the
Red Cross movement.[13]

WFP works closely with UNHCR in both emergencies and during
protracted refugee situations to deliver food to refugee populations.
WFP and UNHCR conduct joint assessment missions to refugee
camps and settlements to ensure that refugees are receiving a sufficient
quantity and diversity of food that is nutritionally balanced and cul-
turally appropriate. WFP provides food assistance to refugee populations of 5,000 or more who are in need of assistance, whereas UNHCR
is responsible for the food needs of smaller groups. The importance of
this partnership has increased over the past decade as a greater
number of host states require refugees to remain in closed camps and
settlements with no opportunities to pursue self-reliance. In such circumstances, refugees are almost entirely dependent on the international community to provide them with the food they need to survive.

As donors have become increasingly reluctant to fund protracted refugee situations, and as the cost of food has risen,[14] UNHCR and WFP have issued numerous joint appeals calling on donors to provide the support necessary to prevent malnutrition in refugee populations.

UNDP is the primary UN agency responsible for development and poverty-reduction activities. The UNDP Representative also typically serves as the UN Resident Coordinator of the UN Country Team in many host countries and countries of origin where UNHCR works. UNDP also represents UNHCR in some ten host countries where UNHCR does not have its own office.

Since the mid-1990s, UNHCR has recognized the important links between solutions to refugee situations and sustainable development.[15] In April 1997, UNDP and UNHCR agreed to cooperate in five key areas. As a consequence of its global presence, UNDP helps UNHCR detect significant population movements, thereby facilitating a more timely and effective response. Once refugee movements have occurred, the two organizations work to mitigate the impact of large refugee populations on local economic, social and environmental conditions in host countries. One of the most significant areas of cooperation between UNDP and UNHCR in recent years has been in the area of conflict resolution, post-conflict reconstruction and peacebuilding in countries with significant displaced populations, including specific programs in countries of origin to support the successful reintegration of returnees. Finally, while the two organizations have agreed to coordinate their activities to help ease the transition from emergency relief to long-term development, significant gaps in this area remain.

While these areas of cooperation are widely recognized as essential preconditions for an effective response to refugee situations, there have been numerous difficulties in the relationship between UNDP and UNHCR over the past decade. Many of these difficulties result from different priorities and programs in the field, stemming from the significant gap that remains between relief and development activities within the UN system. Tensions also arise from the perception that UNHCR is increasingly targeting development assistance budgets to meet its funding gaps, putting UNDP and UNHCR in competition for the same donor funds.

As outlined in Chapter 3, the past decade has witnessed increased cooperation between UNHCR and the peace and security actors of the UN system, especially the Security Council. In operational terms, this shift has resulted in a closer working relationship between UNHCR and DPKO. In April 2004, DPKO and UNHCR co-signed an Inter-Office Memorandum on the importance of the relationship between the two bodies. The memo made reference to the number of operations where UNHCR and DPKO have successfully cooperated—including Kosovo, East Timor, Western Sahara, Afghanistan, and Central and West Africa—and emphasized the important links between effectively responding to forced migration and maintaining international peace and security. Noting that previous cooperation had largely been *ad hoc*, the memo pointed to a number of areas where increased cooperation was both possible and desirable, especially on areas such as disarmament, demobilization and reintegration (DDR) in situations such as Sudan and Burundi.

Since the late 1990s, UNHCR has encouraged DPKO to consider the deployment of personnel to refugee-populated areas to address a range of security concerns relating to refugee movements. However, cooperation between the two agencies in the field remains limited as a result of the specific mandates given to particular peacekeeping missions and the significant challenges of funding, mandate and access faced by UN peacekeepers, especially in situations like Darfur.

IOM is not a UN agency, but an inter-governmental body established to facilitate more orderly migration and the movement of people. Given the numerous areas of overlap between their activities, the working relationship between UNHCR and IOM has a long history marked by both close cooperation and bitter competition. In May 1997, IOM and UNHCR agreed to cooperate in the monitoring and prevention of crisis situations, contingency planning for emergencies and capacity-building. Areas of IOM-UNHCR cooperation have subsequently increased, and now include work with IDPs, the movement of individuals who have not been accepted for asylum, and joint advocacy efforts. IOM also supports UNHCR with a number of logistical functions such as the facilitation of repatriation convoys and the arrangement of travel for refugees being resettled to a third country. IOM also provides other areas of support, such as language training and cultural orientation for resettled refugees.

Despite these important areas of cooperation, competition between the two agencies remains. The perception persists among some UNHCR staff that IOM encroaches upon traditional UNHCR activities. In addition, IOM has been seen by some UNHCR staff to undertake an increasing number of activities, such as the management of regional processing centers, to be contradictory to the principles of international refugee protection.

Finally, UNHCR has a long history of cooperation with all elements of the Red Cross movement, including the International Committee of the Red Cross (ICRC), the International Federation of Red Cross and

Red Crescent Societies (IFRC), and national Red Cross and Red Crescent societies. Established in 1863, the ICRC is the oldest NGO in the world.[16] Like UNHCR, the ICRC works primarily to respond to the human consequences of armed conflict. Through its vast global work in exchanging messages, visiting detainees and facilitating contact between families separated by hostilities, ICRC has made a significant contribution to areas of refugee protection such as family reunification. Traditionally, ICRC's activities with displaced populations dealt mainly with IDPs in countries of origin, whereas UNHCR's primary focus was with refugees in regional host countries. In the 1990s, however, as UNHCR expanded its operations into countries of origin, the work of these two organizations increasingly overlapped. As a result, UNHCR and ICRC have worked in operations as diverse as northern Iraq, Somalia, the former Yugoslavia, Rwanda, Sri Lanka, and East Timor.

Since the Algerian War of Independence in the 1950s and 1960s, UNHCR has also had close working relations with the IFRC. As UNHCR's activities expended into Africa and Asia in the 1960s and 1970s, the IFRC was one of its main implementing partners in a number of refugee emergencies. In fact, the presence of the IFRC in many host countries facilitated UNHCR's access prior to the formal expansion of its geographic mandate. Finally, national Red Cross and Red Crescent Societies are UNHCR's implementing partners in a number of operations, providing support in a range of activities, including health, camp management, and logistics. This relationship is especially important in situations where access for international agencies is either too dangerous or politically difficult.

UNHCR and NGOs

In addition to the Red Cross movement, UNHCR has relied upon NGOs as its main operational partners throughout its existence. In 1953, High Commissioner van Heuven Goedhart noted that "the UNHCR has had the most excellent relations with the voluntary agencies" and that "these agencies deserve that high tributes should be paid to what they and their thousands of collaborators are doing."[17] While UNHCR now works with NGOs in a wide range of capacities, it has two broad categories of partnerships with NGOs. UNHCR has implementing partners, where the Office provides financial support to an NGO to deliver specific programs to refugees, as specified in a formal project agreement. Second, UNHCR has operational partners, where there is voluntary coordination between the Office and an NGO in areas such as emergency relief and refugee resettlement, but where the NGO receives no financial support from UNHCR for the services it delivers.

The number of UNHCR's NGO partners and the scale of their work have increased significantly in recent years. In the mid-1960s, UNHCR had fewer than 20 formal partnerships with NGOs, many of whom were international NGOs. Some 40 years later, UNHCR has concluded project agreements with over 500 NGOs around the world, 80 percent of which are local or national NGOs. Between 1994 and 2003, the Office channeled some US$4 billion of its operational budgets through partners, some US$3 billion of which was through international and national NGOs.[18] In 2003 alone, UNHCR channeled US$340 million, a third of its overall budget, through some 700 partners, of which US$231 million went to 572 NGOs.[19]

NGOs have traditionally supported UNHCR's assistance activities. For example, NGOs such as the International Rescue Committee (IRC), CARE, OXFAM, and the Lutheran World Federation (LWF) are UNHCR's implementing partners in crucial areas such as camp management, water and sanitation and health. This focus on supporting assistance activities over protection functions has stemmed largely from the concern by NGOs that human rights activities are dangerously political, beyond their mandates and compromise their independence and neutrality. In recent years, however, a growing number of NGOs have provided UNHCR with direct support for its core protection functions. For example, the IRC now manages the Protection Surge Capacity Project to ensure that Protection Officers can be deployed to emerging refugee situations, while the International Catholic Migration Commission (ICMC), manages a deployment scheme to send personnel to reinforce UNHCR's refugee resettlement activities. More generally, NGOs such as the IRC, the Danish Refugee Council, and the Norwegian Refugee Council support the Office's emergency response capacity by maintaining stand-by arrangement for rapid deployment.

The increasing scope and scale of UNHCR activities implemented by NGOs are both encouraging and problematic. The involvement of such a range of NGOs, especially local and national NGOs, suggests that an important contribution is being made to local capacity-building. At the same time, the involvement of NGOs in the planning and delivery of protection and assistance to refugees is an important counter-balance to the interests of states and the pressures faced by UNHCR. However, an increasing number of non-UNHCR staff and volunteers in the field are doing work in the Office's core mandate activities of protection and solutions often without sufficient training or guidance. In 2006, for example, some 14 percent of UNHCR staff in the field were UN volunteers.[20] These developments raise important questions about the priorities of UNHCR, as evidenced in staffing allocations, and the question of accountability when UNHCR fails to fulfill its mandate in such field situations.

NGOs have also become increasingly important partners in the development of UNHCR policies and priorities.[21] Since the mid-1980s, UNHCR has held formal consultations with NGOs immediately prior to annual ExCom meetings. These consultations run over several days, include more than 200 representatives from more than 150 NGOs, and allow NGOs and UNHCR to discuss a wide range of policy and operational issues of common concern. Working through the Geneva-based International Council of Voluntary Agencies (ICVA), NGOs have also lobbied to become increasingly involved in on-going policy discussions between UNHCR and states. NGOs have sought to make these traditionally bilateral discussions more tripartite, and to provide NGOs with a forum to contribute their perspective. For example, UNHCR, resettlement countries and resettlement NGOs have held Annual Tripartite Consultations on Resettlement since the late 1990s. NGO leadership in these meetings has specifically led to more formal agreements on the reception and integration of resettled refugees.

UNHCR's relationship with donors and the politics of funding

By far the most important relationship for UNHCR, however, remains its relationship with donor countries. Since its creation, UNHCR has faced the challenge of how to fund its work. According to its 1950 Statute:

> no expenditure other than administrative expenditures relating to the functioning of the Office of the High Commissioner shall be borne on the budget of the United Nations and all other expenditures relating to the activities of the High Commissioner shall be financed by voluntary contributions.[22]

In the early days of the Office, when its work was primarily focused on legal protection in Europe, UNHCR operated on a very modest budget. It was not until the global expansion of the Office in the 1970s and 1980s that UNHCR's budget began to increase dramatically. UNHCR's budget peaked in 1994 when its requirements exceeded US $1.4 billion, primarily because of refugee emergencies in the former

Yugoslavia, the African Great Lakes and elsewhere. Since then, UNHCR's budget has remained relatively constant at approximately US$1 billion per year.[23] Given this dramatic increase in the organization's budget over the past 55 years, contributions from the UN Regular Budget now account for less than 3 percent of UNHCR's Annual Budget. As a result, UNHCR is almost exclusively dependent on voluntary contributions to carry out its programs.

The fact that UNHCR has no permanent funding has a number of significant implications for the organization. For example, it makes multi-year planning exceptionally difficult. In any given year, UNHCR cannot predict what funds it will have available for particular programs. As such, engagement in areas that require multi-year commitments, such as development and rehabilitation for returning refugee populations, are very difficult. UNHCR can never be certain when and if its budget will be fully met. The organization is consequently in a frequent state of crisis, often leading to cutbacks and program closures towards the end of the budgetary years.

In response, UNHCR must dedicate considerable time and effort to fundraising and donor relations. This emphasis is compounded by the fact that funding has tended to come from a relatively small number of so-called traditional donors, with around three-quarters of its budget coming from its top ten donors (Figure 4.2). The unpredictability of funding and the concentration of donorship have placed UNHCR in a precarious political position. On the one hand, it has attempted to safeguard the integrity of its mandate by being seen to be politically impartial. On the other hand, its existence and ability to carry out its programs have been dependent upon its ability to respond to the interests of a relatively small number of donor states.

Each year, UNHCR's Annual Programme Budget is approved by ExCom. In order to raise money for the Annual Programme Budget, UNHCR publishes its Global Appeal each December, setting out its strategic priorities and specific program needs for the year. The Office then convenes an annual pledging conference, at which donors commit to fund activities. Where unforeseen needs arise during the year, additional programs can be authorized by the High Commissioner after ExCom has met, and these form part of the Supplementary Programme Budget. Money for these supplementary programs is raised through special appeals.

When contributing to UNHCR's various budgets, however, states may specify how, where and on what basis their contributions may be used by the Office. This practice, known as "earmarking," remains common (Figure 4.3). In 2006, 53 percent of contributions to UNHCR

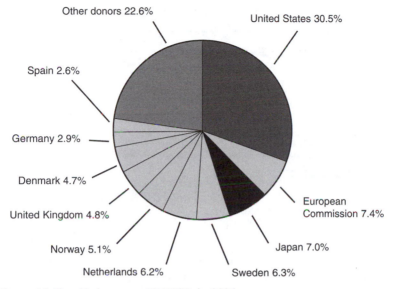

Figure 4.2 Top 10 donors to UNHCR in 2006.
Source: UNHCR Global Report (2006).

were "tightly earmarked" for specific countries and activities, while 28 percent were "lightly earmarked" for specific geographical regions and only 20 percent came with no restrictions.[24]

Some states have used earmarking more than others. For example, the US, the European Commission and Japan exclusively earmark, while the Scandinavian states and the Netherlands have traditionally earmarked to a far lesser extent. The advantage of allowing earmarking, rather than insisting on the common pooling of all contributions, is that it creates an incentive for states to contribute to UNHCR's work, albeit for partly self-interested reasons.[25] This is because it allows them to prioritize the allocation of their funding in ways that simultaneously meet the donor states' own strategic aims.[26] However, the disadvantage for UNHCR of earmarking is that it makes contributions highly selective, and means they are often based on states' interests rather than refugees' needs.

The practice of earmarking also makes donations far less predictable and less coherent, over time and in relation to one another. In fact, earmarking allows donors to exercise considerable influence over the work of UNHCR as programs considered important by donors receive considerable support, while those deemed less important receive less support. For example, during the late 1990s, while the international community

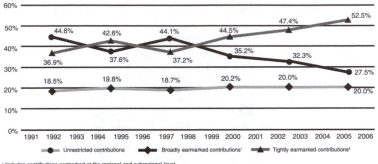

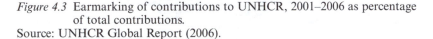

Figure 4.3 Earmarking of contributions to UNHCR, 2001–2006 as percentage of total contributions.
Source: UNHCR Global Report (2006).

focused attention and resources on the crises in Kosovo and East Timor, conflict and displacement in Africa were virtually ignored. This pattern continues almost a decade later as donor governments still give vastly disproportionate amounts of aid to a few well-known crises and trivial amounts of aid to dozens of other refugee programs.

Understanding the motives underlying why, and on what basis, states donate to UNHCR is a complex question. Most states seem to contribute to refugee protection because of a combination of norms and interests.[27] Formal norms such as the 1951 Convention play a role in shaping a sense of states' obligation towards refugees. Meanwhile, less formal norms such as UNHCR's ExCom Conclusions on issues such as burden sharing or a generalized sense of moral obligation towards refugees may guide some states to support UNHCR more than others. However, states have rarely contributed to UNHCR for purely altruistic reasons. Rather, they have generally been at least partly guided by their own perceived interests. Statistical analysis of earmarked contributions by European states shows a correlation between the host states of asylum for which states were earmarked and a range of donor interests. States such as the UK, Belgium, and France, for example, earmarked partly on the basis of history of receiving asylum seekers from a particular state and their historical connections to the states through, for example, colonialism or foreign policy.[28] Meanwhile, analysis of donors' financial or in-kind contributions in conferences and processes such as ICARA, the CPA, CIREFCA, and Convention Plus, as discussed in Chapters 2 and 3, highlights how Northern donors' contributions towards refugee protection in the

South have been motivated by strategic concerns in linked areas such as foreign policy, security, migration, and trade relations, often more than by a concern for refugees protection *per se.*[29]

The fact that donors largely contribute to UNHCR on the basis of their own perceived interests makes the concentration of donors all the more problematic. This is because it means that the interests of a relatively small number of states are highly influential in determining UNHCR's activities. In 2006, the top ten donors were the United States, the European Commission, Japan, Sweden, the Netherlands, Norway, the UK, Denmark, Germany, and Spain, with all other countries accounting for less than a quarter of contributions to UNHCR. This has given these donor states a disproportionate influence over UNHCR's activities.

The most influential of all donor states, however, remains the United States. For decades, the United States has been by far the biggest donor in absolute terms, consistently providing more than 30 percent of UNHCR's budget. In many ways, the United States represents the global hegemon within the refugee regime. Because of its size and relative power,[30] coupled with the role that refugees have played in US foreign policy since the Second World War,[31] the United States has been willing to disproportionately fund the world's refugee protection regime. While the scale of US support has enabled UNHCR to carry out many of its programs, American dominance has enabled Washington to determine many policy and personnel decisions within UNHCR.

The significant role played by a small number of donors and their interests places UNHCR in a challenging political position. On the one hand, the Office needs to have independent influence on the behavior of states in order to fulfill its mandate responsibilities for the protection of refugees. On the other hand, UNHCR needs to attract voluntary contributions to pursue its work, and must therefore be seen to be relevant to its key donors and capable of responding to their concerns. Reconciling the need to have an autonomous influence on states with being responsive to donor interests has been a precarious balancing act for the Office. At many stages in its history it has placed UNHCR on a "perilous path," navigating between states' interests and the norms that it seeks to uphold.[32]

During the 1990s, for example, UNHCR sought to attract additional voluntary contributions to enable it to grow as an organization, expanding its mandate, staff and budget by taking on a number of high profile roles in the Balkans and the African Great Lakes. As outlined in Chapter 3, however, UNHCR was frustrated by its inability to be fully effective in Bosnia and the former Zaire. As a result of

UNHCR's performance in these situations, donors subsequently reduced their contributions to the organization. In addition, the perception that the Office had been instrumentally used to meet the interests of its major donors in ways that contradicted its core mandate damaged the legitimacy and moral authority of UNHCR.

Moreover, the belief that UNHCR is beholden to a relatively small number of Northern donors has also had an impact on the way the Office is often perceived by Southern states. Under Lubbers, the Office again attempted to make itself relevant to its key donors. Recognizing that many European states, in particular, were adopting increasingly restrictive practices towards spontaneous arrival asylum seekers in the context of their wider concern to manage immigration, Lubbers conceived the notion of Convention Plus, as outlined in Chapter 3. The initiative's main supporters were the European Commission, Denmark, the Netherlands, and the UK. The perception that Convention Plus was a European donor-led initiative conceived to meet a migration-management agenda undermined its credibility in the eyes of many Southern states.[33]

The challenge of relevance and the need to recognize and respond to states' interests are greater now than ever. The emergence of a number of new humanitarian actors has meant that UNHCR now faces increasing competition from other actors prepared to work as implementing partners on behalf of states. As a result, it is increasingly possible for states to bypass UNHCR and instead use a range of other actors and forums in order to meet their interests. For example, IOM offers a range of services to states, some of which overlap with UNHCR's traditional work in areas such as repatriation. Increasingly asylum is being addressed through regional bodies such as the European Commission or informal networks such as the Intergovernmental Consultations on Asylum and Migration (IGC).

In an attempt to address the disproportionate influence of a limited number of donor states, UNHCR has started to look for alternative sources of voluntary contributions. For example, UNHCR has identified multinational corporations and private foundations as potential sources of funding. In 2006, UNHCR created a Private Sector Fund Raising Section, based in the Division of External Relations. That year, it raised a total of US$21.7 million in voluntary donations from firms, foundations, and NGOs. Although it is questionable what scope this type of appeal has, and what motives different private actors might have for contributing to UNHCR, the private sector may open up a new avenue for expanding UNHCR's sources of funding. The Office may be able to learn from the expanding literature on other areas of governance in which the private sector has already played a prominent role.[34]

UNHCR has been working in recent years to encourage so-called non-traditional donors to contribute to its work. States such as China, Brazil, Mexico, Saudi Arabia, Jordan, South Korea, Indonesia, the Philippines, for example, may have the means to make a considerable contribution to funding UNHCR, while reducing the current concentration of donors. China's emerging interest in development and humanitarianism in Africa, for example, may represent an unexplored but potentially interesting opportunity for UNHCR if it can be channeled into a greater commitment to refugee protection.

These efforts notwithstanding, UNHCR's ability to attract funds remains a political issue. The Office has historically been most successful in fundraising not in situations in which it has adopted a technocratic approach to programming and appeal, but where it has been politically engaged and has recognized the challenges and opportunities presented at a particular historical juncture. The success of initiatives such as CIREFCA in attracting additional donor contributions was based on recognizing and engaging with the wider context of states' interests at the time, and then demonstrating the leadership to persuade states that those wider interests could be met through a commitment to refugee protection. The era of globalization and the post-9/11 context present both challenges and opportunities for UNHCR's donor relations. To be successful in reconciling donor relevance with a commitment to the integrity of its mandate, UNHCR's donor relations must incorporate an ability to recognize and engage with the broader political context within which donors make decisions to meet their interests through UNHCR. Concerns with terrorism, security, and migration control now dominate the concerns of donor states. Serving these interests uncritically risks the integrity of UNHCR's mandate; but ignoring them risks UNHCR being bypassed.

More generally, the forces of globalization present UNHCR with a number of challenges and opportunities. As outlined in this chapter, UNHCR's place within the UN system, its internal dynamics and structures, and its relationship with a wide range of external actors have all changed in response to developments in the international system. Given that these relationships will face additional pressures in the future as the nature of displacement continues to change, UNHCR will need to continually adapt to remain relevant. At the same time, however, the changing humanitarian landscape begs important questions about the scope and continued relevance of UNHCR's core mandate functions of protection and solutions for refugees.

5 Protection, solutions, and UNHCR's core mandate

UNHCR was established by states to serve two core purposes: (1) to ensure the international protection of refugees; and (2) to find a solution to their plight. To carry out these responsibilities, the Office primarily relies on the authority of a number of core instruments, including UNHCR's Statute, the 1951 Convention and its 1967 Protocol. While adherence to these core instruments is essential to the work of UNHCR, they have been under considerable strain in recent years. A growing number of states, in both the North and South, have questioned the continued relevance of these core instruments, especially the 1951 Convention. Critics have argued that the 1951 Convention is Euro-centric, inflexible, outdated, and not capable of addressing the complexities of today's global refugee crisis. States now point to a number of contemporary challenges left unaddressed by the 1951 Convention, such as the changing nature of asylum, the mixing of asylum seekers and economic migrants, the range of security concerns associated with refugee movements, the costs to states associated with granting asylum, and the growing scale and globalization of the problem of forced migrants. In contrast, supporters of the 1951 Convention, including UNHCR, argue that while the Convention is not perfect, it continues to provide an important and legitimate foundation for the international refugee protection regime.

These challenges to the core instruments of refugee protection raise important questions about the scope and continued relevance of UNHCR's core mandate. As outlined in earlier chapters, significant gaps in the international refugee protection regime do exist, and there have been a number of occasions when UNHCR has not been able to fulfill its mandate. The increasingly restrictive nature of asylum policies in the North and South highlights the gaps in UNHCR's ability to fulfill the protection aspects of its mandate. Likewise, the increasingly protracted nature of refugee situations around the world underlines the difficulties experienced by UNHCR in fulfilling its responsibility to find solutions for refugees. Finally, the rising importance of IDPs, and the on-going debate within the international community relating to the responsibility to provide protection to this group, have added new salience to old debates on the appropriate scope of UNHCR's mandate.

UNHCR's ability to fulfill its core mandate responsibilities has been increasingly challenged by the actions of states, the changing international humanitarian environment and the changing nature of forced displacement. As the categories of displaced persons have increased in recent years, the international community has come under pressure to identify who will be responsible for ensuring that displaced people are protected. Since UNHCR is the only UN agency with a clear protection mandate, the Office has been increasingly expected to assume this expanded responsibility. While UNHCR has recently sought to demonstrate its relevance by assuming this expanded role, important questions remain about the impact of this decision on the future of refugee protection in the twenty-first century. This chapter therefore analyses the central aspects of the Office's core mandate and the challenges that the Office faces in attempting to fulfill this role.

Core instruments of refugee protection

As detailed in Chapter 1, the principal instruments of refugee protection are the UNHCR's Statute and the 1951 Convention. The Statute not only specifies the core mandate responsibilities of UNHCR but also details the possible solutions for refugees, namely repatriation to their country of origin, integration in the host country, or resettlement to a third country.[1] Likewise, the 1951 Convention defines who qualifies for refugee status and specifies a number of mechanisms by which certain individuals could either be excluded from refugee status or have their refugee status revoked.[2] The bulk of the Convention specifies the social, economic and political rights to be afforded to individuals recognized as refugees. Perhaps the most significant right afforded to refugees by the Convention is protection against *refoulement*. As specified in Article 33(1) of the 1951 Convention:

> No Contracting State shall expel or return ("refouler") a refugee in any manner whatsoever to the frontiers of territories where his life or freedom would be threatened on account of his race, religion, nationality, membership of a particular social group or political opinion.

Despite the significance of the 1951 Convention as the cornerstone of the international community's commitment to refugee protection, its shortcomings were recognized from the very beginning. Decolonization in Africa and Asia brought a significant number of new states into the international community. Many of these states considered the 1951 Convention to be irrelevant to their situation, given that the refugee definition was limited to European refugees resulting from events prior to 1951.[3] Many new states in Africa and Asia also noted that the Convention was based on a highly individualized notion of persecution and did not reflect the emerging refugee crises in their regions, which were characterized by generalized violence and mass flight. Finally, the 1951 Convention provided no guidance on how the costs of granting asylum to refugees should be shared by the international community—so-called burden sharing.

In response to these concerns, and in light of the changing operational realities outlined in Chapter 2, UNHCR promoted the 1967 Protocol, which removed the temporal and geographic limitation on the refugee definition. Notwithstanding this development, some states continued to believe that the 1951 Convention did not fully respond to the nature of the refugee problem in their region, prompting a number of regional organizations, such as the OAU, to adopt additional regional instruments designed to supplement the 1951 Convention and the 1967 Protocol. The existence of these regional instruments does not, however, limit the authority of the 1951 Convention or the 1967 Protocol. As of 1 December 2006, 147 states were party to one or both of these instruments,[4] making the 1951 Convention and the 1967 Protocol the recognized legal foundations of the international refugee protection regime.

Challenges to refugee protection in the North and South

Since the 1990s, there has been a dramatic shift in state behavior away from observance of the principles of the 1951 Convention in both the North and South, placing incredible strain on UNHCR and the international refugee protection regime. In the North, the period since the end of the Cold War has been marked by a shift "from asylum to containment,"[5] where Western states have largely limited the asylum they offer to refugees and have focused on efforts to contain refugees in their region of origin. In the South, which continues to host the vast majority of the world's refugees, states are also responding to the mass arrival and prolonged presence of refugees by placing limits on the quantity and quality of asylum they offer. The result is a global crisis of asylum.

The asylum crisis in the North originated in the 1980s when the number of asylum seekers arriving in developed countries from conflicts in Africa, Asia, the Caribbean, Central America, and the Middle East began to rise significantly. For example, asylum applications in Western Europe rose from 20,000 in 1976 to 450,000 in 1990. While this rise in numbers is clearly significant, some commentators have rightfully concluded that "rising asylum claims tell us what governments have been reacting to, but they do not tell us why governments have grasped with such alacrity measures designed to restrict and prevent rather than include and manage those striving for asylum."[6] More significant was the fact that the majority of these asylum seekers came from developing countries, many of whom had traveled to the North with false documents and with the help of smugglers. At the same time, large numbers of illegal migrants used asylum channels to gain entry to Western countries. In response, Western states introduced a series of measures to reduce the number of individuals seeking asylum on their territory. These measures included non-arrival policies, such as carrier sanctions and visa requirements, diversion policies, such as safe-third country agreements, an increasingly restrictive application of the 1951 Convention, and a range of deterrent policies, such as detention of asylum seekers and the denial of social assistance. Over a period of some 20 years, Western states have systematically eroded the principle and practice of asylum to the point where some states, like the UK, have openly called for the scrapping of the 1951 Convention and a new international refugee regime, premised on containing refugees within their region of origin.[7] After the 9/11 terrorist attacks in the United States, asylum policies in the North were exacerbated by heightened security concerns and became linked to the so-called global war on terror.

These moves to contain refugees in their regions of origin, coupled with a rise in global refugee numbers in the early 1990s and the problematic response by the international community, have placed a significant strain on asylum countries in the South, especially in Africa and Asia. As refugee numbers continued to rise in the 1990s, states in the developing world began to also place restrictions on asylum. Some states limited the quantity of asylum they offered to refugees, by closing their borders to prevent arrivals, by pushing for the early and often unsustainable return of refugees to their country of origin, and, in exceptional cases, forcibly expelling entire refugee populations. More generally, states have been placing limits on the quality of asylum they offer to refugees, by denying them the social and economic rights contained in the 1951 Convention, such as freedom of movement and the right to seek employment. Many states in the South now require refugees to remain in isolated and insecure refugee camps, cut off from the local community, and fully dependent on dwindling international assistance.

UNHCR's response

The crisis of asylum in both the North and South has confronted UNHCR with a nearly impossible task. While mandated by the international community to ensure the protection of refugees and to find solutions to their plight, UNHCR cannot realize this mandate without the cooperation of states. As the global crisis of asylum emerged, states largely excluded UNHCR and increasingly devised their own responses to insulate themselves from the growing number of refugees seeking access to their territories. The lack of cooperation by states, coupled with the global impasse between Northern donor countries and Southern host states, has significantly frustrated UNHCR's activities in recent years. As noted in Chapter 3, states have become increasingly disillusioned with the 1951 Convention and a number of gaps have emerged in the protection framework.

In response to these developments and in an attempt to narrow the gap between the protection needs of refugees and the interests of states, UNHCR initiated the Global Consultations on International Protection. A primary concern for UNHCR has been that a significant number of refugee-hosting states, especially in Asia, have not yet signed the 1951 Convention, while a greater number of states who have signed the Convention continue to apply it in a restrictive way. A major focus of the Global Consultations process was therefore to encourage greater respect for the core instruments of the international refugee protection regime. UNHCR called upon all states to sign the 1951 Convention and for states that are party to Convention to develop better procedures to ensure its implementation.

Through the Global Consultations process, UNHCR also tried to address the longstanding and difficult task of burden sharing. While the importance of international solidarity to share the costs associated with granting asylum are expressed in a range of international documents, from the Preamble of the 1951 Convention, General Assembly resolutions and a significant number of ExCom Conclusions over the past 25 years, international law does not include a duty on states to engage in burden sharing. Rather the global refugee regime has been characterized by burden shifting with some states bearing more of the burden—whether in numbers of refugees hosted or in financial contributions—than others. Many observers, however, have noted that burden sharing is an essential precondition for an effective international refugee protection regime.

As with previous efforts to address the absence of burden-sharing obligations, UNHCR was not able to gain support for a structured, pre-negotiated approach to burden sharing through the Global Consultations process. Instead, the outcomes of the Consultations simply proposed a series of activities to strengthen the protection capacities of countries of first asylum, to enhance UNHCR's partnerships with NGOs and civil society, to empower refugee communities to meet their own protection needs, and for resettlement to be used more effectively as a tool of burden sharing. None of these proposed activities, however, comprehensively engaged with the core concerns of major host states in the South who are the principal proponents of effective burden-sharing mechanism.

Another major concern of host states in Africa and Asia that UNHCR tried to address through the Consultations was the impact of refugee movements on local, national and regional security. Refugee movements have had security implications throughout the twentieth century. In some instances, refugee movements have had a direct impact on state security, particularly when armed elements are based in refugee camps, when refugee movements cause a spill-over of conflict into neighboring states, or when the presence of refugee groups exacerbates tensions between states. The presence of refugees can also cause more indirect security concerns, especially when refugees compete with host populations for access to jobs, social services and natural resources, when the presence of refugees may exacerbate local tensions within a host country, and when the arrival of refugees leads to an increase in crime and insecurity.

UNHCR has been trying to address this broad range of security concerns for more than a decade, not only through the Global Consultations, but also through discussions with other UN agencies and actors, as outlined in Chapter 3. While the outcomes of the Global Consultations recognized the potentially important role of the broader UN system in addressing these challenges, the process resulted only in a series of recommendations which focused exclusively on the physical security of refugees in refugee camps. Given the regional and fluid nature of insecurity in the developing world, however, this refugee-specific approach to security issues did not address the fundamental security concerns of host states in Africa and Asia.

In recent years, UNHCR has also developed a more acute awareness of the particular needs of refugee women and children. Women and children account for some 80 percent of the world's refugees.

UNHCR and NGOs have developed numerous guidelines and policies to ensure their protection but neither sufficient resources nor enough attention has been given to the protection of this refugee group. In an effort to address these shortcomings, UNHCR has frequently highlighted the particular needs of refugee women and children, and called for the implementation of a range of measures to improve their protection. Despite the Office's efforts, this group continues to be among the world's most vulnerable refugees.

Another focus for UNHCR in recent years has been efforts to respond to state concerns about the so-called asylum–migration nexus. Recognizing that refugees often move within broader groups of migrants, not all of whom may be in need of international protection, UNHCR has called for better identification of refugees and asylum seekers, greater efforts to combat smuggling and trafficking, the reduction of irregular or secondary movements of refugees, and a range of other activities designed to protect refugees within the context of broader migration management programs. Critics have argued that UNHCR's desire to demonstrate its relevance in responding to Northern states' concerns has caused it to compromise on a number of protection principles and distance itself from host states in the South.

While UNHCR has engaged in a range of campaigns and activities in recent years to address this broad spectrum of protection challenges, its overall impact remains limited. Since its inception, UNHCR has been dependent on states to fund its work to address shortcomings in refugee protection. The Office's ability to ensure refugee protection is also dependent on the cooperation of states in the North and South, many of whom are retreating from the core objectives of refugee protection. These concerns led some participants during the Global Consultations to question whether UNHCR was capable of exercising its supervisory responsibility under Article 31 of the 1951 Convention.[8] Indeed, some experts have recommended that an independent committee be established with the responsibility of overseeing state observance of their obligations under the 1951 Convention. While UNHCR needs to strengthen its supervisory role, the Office remains trapped between the principles it was created to uphold and the limited influence it wields in its relationship with states. So long as this tension remains, UNHCR's ability to fundamentally address shortcomings in refugee protection will be limited.

Internally displaced persons (IDPs)

While addressing the gaps in the protection of refugees, UNHCR has simultaneously been confronted with the task of protecting an entirely new category of forced migrants, namely IDPs. International concern for IDPs has grown significantly in recent years. IDPs are commonly defined as "persons in a refugee-like situation who have not crossed the borders of their country." Internal displacement can be caused by conflict, environmental disaster, economic change or large-scale development projects. However, the IDP debate as a whole, and UNHCR's role, have generally focused on those displaced by conflict. It is estimated that in 2007 there were around 25 million IDPs compared to the roughly 10 million refugees. In recent years, UNHCR has engaged in IDP protection in a range of situations—most notably in Colombia, Sudan, Azerbaijan, Liberia, Sri Lanka, the Russian Federation, the Former Yugoslav Republics, Georgia, and Afghanistan.[9]

Like refugees, IDPs have been displaced from their homes and are in need of protection. However, they have historically not received the same rights and opportunities as refugees. While there has been a relatively clear legal and institutional framework regulating refugee protection, the IDP issue was rarely recognized or debated until the end of the 1980s, and the international regime governing IDP protection and assistance only began to take shape in the 1990s. Since the early 1990s, a Special Representative of the Secretary-General for IDPs has been appointed, a set of Guiding Principles on Internal Displacement has been compiled and widely endorsed by states, and a new institutional framework has begun to emerge.[10]

Historically, the distinction between refugees and IDPs has been based on the principle of state sovereignty. As the central tenet of international law, sovereignty has been taken to imply the territorial integrity of states and the acceptance of the principle of non-intervention in the internal affairs of states. Consequently, border crossing has been a central distinguishing feature for two main reasons. Unlike in the case of refugees who have lost the protection of their home government, with IDPs, the bond between citizen and state is never entirely severed. Consequently, the primary responsibility for protecting its own population continues to rest with the home state. To undermine the principle would go against the basis of human rights law which is about the relationship of a state to its own citizens. In addition, unlike refugees, IDPs are not necessarily within reach of international assistance. Consequently, there has been a practical obstacle to protection which does not exist where border crossing takes place.

Because of these widely acknowledged differences, determining which actors have responsibility for IDP protection and assistance has been complex and challenging. Within this wider context, there has been extensive debate about what UNHCR's role should be, and under what conditions it should be involved in the protection and assistance of IDPs. During the past decade and a half, the Office's role in IDP protection has gradually grown and its mandate has broadened to include a growing proportion of the world's IDPs. From an initially very *ad hoc* and selective role, IDP protection has become an increasingly central and systematic part of UNHCR's work. Yet, this has been a controversial shift. Some believe that taking on such a role risks undermining UNHCR's traditional mandate, while others believe that the need is sufficiently great and UNHCR has the necessary expertise. Which of these opposing views is the case will depend upon how well the Office addresses the range of political and practical challenges that emerge from its involvement in IDP protection and assistance.

UNHCR's evolving role in IDP protection

IDP protection was not part of UNHCR's original mandate. Article 9 of UNHCR's 1950 Statute, however, allows for the possibility that, over time, this mandate might be extended if authorized by the General Assembly and if sufficient funds were available. In the early years of UNHCR's work, the organization was able to selectively assist those who did not qualify as 1951 Convention refugees either by recognizing them as *prima facie* refugees or by using General Assembly resolutions to assist those who did not fall directly within the mandate of UNHCR. Through this means, UNHCR occasionally offered protection to those people it described as "displaced persons" when refugee protection or repatriation operations made it "operationally untenable" not to. The Office provided protection to the internally displaced in, for example, Sudan in 1972, Guinea-Bissau, Angola and Mozambique in 1974, and Vietnam and Laos in 1975.[11]

The end of the Cold War was important for opening opportunities for IDP protection. This is partly because the end of a bipolar world led to the emerging consensus that state sovereignty was no longer inviolable and that, under certain conditions, intervention might be a valid means to protect human rights. The turning point in the IDP debate came in northern Iraq in 1991, when the Security Council authorized the creation of "safe havens" for internally displaced Kurds as part of Operation Provide Comfort. High Commissioner Sadako Ogata made the decision to engage UHHCR as the lead agency in providing IDP protection. This was highly controversial within UNHCR because the provision of an "internal flight alternative" was perceived to legitimize Turkey's refusal to open its borders to fleeing Kurds and to deny asylum to bona-fide refugees.

After playing this role in northern Iraq, UNHCR continued to play an *ad hoc* role in a number of humanitarian emergencies, and an increasing number of IDPs became "persons of concern" to UNHCR. The criteria for UNHCR's involvement in IDP protection evolved during the 1990s through an initial General Assembly resolution in 1993 and then a series of internal guidelines and ExCom conclusions. The main criteria to emerge were that, first, there should be a specific request for UNHCR involvement by the Secretary-General; second, that the host state should provide consent; third, that access and security should be guaranteed; fourth, that UNHCR should have the necessary expertise and funds. Finally, a so-called link criterion emerged, whereby for UNHCR to be involved in IDP protection and assistance, it must have a clear relationship to UNHCR's mandate. For example, for UNHCR to be involved, the situation of the IDP population would have to be related to returnees, have the same root causes as a refugee movement, or have the potential to become a cross-border movement. These criteria allowed UNHCR to avoid a formal commitment, while providing the flexibility to get involved in IDP protection when it met UNHCR's political and budgetary needs.[12]

The 1990s also saw the emergence of a legal and normative framework regulating states' responses to IDPs.[13] This began with the appointment of Francis Deng as the Representative of the Secretary-General on Internally Displaced Persons in 1992. Aside from working to raise the profile of the issue through numerous visits to IDP situations, the Representative's work initially focused on the development of a legal and normative framework for IDP protection. This involved the analysis, compilation and synthesis of existing laws as a means to create soft law through the restatement of existing state commitments.[14] Emerging from this process, the Guiding Principles on Internal Displacement were finalized and presented to the Commission on Human Rights in 1998. The Guiding Principles were based mainly on international human rights law and also drew upon international humanitarian law. They provided a formal and authoritative definition of IDPs as

> [people] who have been forced or obliged to flee or to leave their homes or places of habitual residence in particular as a result of generalized violence, violations of human rights or natural or man-made disasters, and who have not crossed an internationally recognized state border.[15]

Following the elaboration of the Guiding Principles, there was significant debate about what would be the appropriate institutional framework to regulate their implementation, and what role UNHCR should play within this structure. The initial suggestion, that UNHCR should be the single agency responsible for IDP protection and assistance, was rejected. Instead, the majority of states preferred the continuation of the prevailing "collaborative" approach, based on inter-agency coordination across the entire UN structure. This approach made IDP protection and assistance part of the overall coordination mechanism for humanitarian affairs. This structure was coordinated by the UN Emergency Relief Coordinator. Different agencies such as WFP, UNICEF and UNHCR could then be called upon to provide expertise and support in different areas of IDP assistance and protection.[16]

In order to assist the collaborative approach, an OCHA Office for IDP Coordination was created in 2001. Furthermore, a Global IDP Database was established by the Norwegian Refugee Council to provide monitoring and surveillance of the emerging IDP regime. At the field level, coordination was provided by the UN Resident Representative. UNHCR's role in this emerging collaborative approach of the early 1990s was as a part of this *ad hoc* and UN system-wide response. At the same time, the Office continued to act where action was in line with its own criteria for involvement and was coordinated through OCHA.[17]

However, the collaborative approach did not always lead to coherent policies or to consistent, predictable responses. Action tended to rely upon a single state or group of states having a strong unilateral interest in getting involved, as was the case in Afghanistan in 2001, for example. More broadly-based multilateral action tended to be highly selective and limited. Coordination between headquarters and field-level was also not always coherent, with different actors engaged at the different levels. The inadequacies of the collaborative approach led to growing debate on how the institutional framework for IDP protection and assistance could be improved. From 2005, the collaborative approach was therefore replaced by the so-called clustered approach. For the first time, the approach set out a clear division of responsibility among the various UN agencies, removing some of the uncertainty and ambiguity of different agencies' roles. For example, the WFP took on responsibility for food and nutrition and UNICEF took on responsibility for child protection. Meanwhile, UNHCR took on three areas of responsibility: protection, camp coordination and management, and shelter.

The clustered approach represented a significant new departure for UNHCR. For the first time it gave UNHCR formal institutional responsibility for IDP protection. This shift in the role of UNHCR was signaled by High Commissioner Antònio Guterres' vision of UNHCR as "a protection organization." Guterres recognized that for UNHCR to have ongoing relevance in a world in which refugees were a declining proportion of the world's displaced people, it would need to expand its focus and apply its expertise in protection beyond working with refugees. He indicated that UNHCR was willing to take on this expanded mandate only insofar as funding from IDP protection would be separate from and additional to funding for refugee protection. However, with no additional staff or guarantees of funding to take on this added responsibility, the great challenge is how to ensure that UNHCR's expanded role in IDP protection does not undermine its role in refugee protection.

UNHCR and IDPs: challenges and controversies

The debate on whether, and if so to what extent, UNHCR should play a role in IDP protection has been highly controversial and elicited strong opinions on both sides of the debate. Many academics and policy-makers see the expansion in role as positive and necessary, while others have argued that it is an example of how UNHCR has been instrumentally used by states to reduce refugee movements. In attempting to reconcile its expanded role in IDP protection with its traditional refugee protection mandate, UNHCR has faced and will continue to face challenges on both a political and a practical level.

In terms of the political challenges, it is clear that many states who have actively argued for improved IDP protection have been concerned to limit the possibility that humanitarian emergencies will lead to those displaced crossing borders and seeking asylum. Where states have pushed the UN system to develop a better legal and institutional framework for IDP protection, this has not always been motivated by purely altruistic reasons but rather a desire to address the underlying causes of refugee movements or to use in-country protection as a substitute for asylum.

This recognition has led to academics, policy-makers and practitioners taking very different perspectives. Some have argued that given the overwhelming need to provide protection to IDPs, and UNHCR's expertise in this area, UNHCR should certainly be taking on this role.[18] From this point of view, the motives of states supporting and funding IDP protection are not as important as the outcome if this leads to enhanced protection and assistance. Others have argued against UNHCR's expanded role in IDP protection, believing that, in going beyond its original mandate, the Office risks becoming politicized in a manner that may conflict with and undermine refugee protection.[19]

Indeed, a number of UNHCR's experiences of IDP protection during the 1990s highlight the dangers of UNHCR being instrumentally used by states. In situations such as Iraq, Bosnia and Somalia, the reluctance of the international community to address root causes led to emergency relief operations led by UNHCR. In these situations, so-called "safety zones," "humanitarian corridors," and "safe havens" were established as tools through which states were able to provide in-country protection and to limit the possibility of a refugee exodus.[20] The difficulty with such approaches is that they often failed to provide adequate protection for the populations to which assistance was provided. In Bosnia, for example, the six UN "safe areas" established in 1993 under the UN Protection Force (UNPROFOR) failed to ensure the security of those displaced, culminating most notably in the Srebrenica massacre. One observer has argued that playing such a role in in-country protection led to the subversion and instrumentalization of UNHCR in ways that undermined its ability to fulfill its core mandate.[21]

There is evidently a risk that UNHCR will be used by states as a political tool for containment in ways that may contradict with and undermine its core mandate. However, the failures of the 1990s are not necessarily an argument that UNHCR should abdicate involvement in IDP protection. Rather, they point to the need for the Office to learn from those past lessons. In particular, UNHCR needs to engage in IDP protection in ways that ensure it is not used either as a substitute for asylum or for political solutions that address root causes. In order to avoid the erosion of its refugee protection mandate and a repeat of its earlier mistakes, UNHCR needs to become more aware of its political environment and ensure that it recognizes the opportunities, constraints and risks that emerge from states' interests. As with refugee protection, states will not engage in IDP protection unless they have a perceived interest. The political challenge, then, is to ensure that these interests are channeled in ways that provide genuine protection to IDPs, while simultaneously safeguarding UNHCR's legitimacy and core mandate.

Protracted refugee situations and the challenge of solutions

As UNHCR decides on the future direction of its work with IDPs, it needs to be mindful of its ability to independently fulfill the second half of its mandate: to find solutions to the plight of refugees. As noted above, UNHCR's Statute outlines three possible solutions for refugees: (1) they may repatriate to their country of origin; (2) they may locally integrate in the host society; or (3) they may be resettled to a third country. While UNHCR's approach to these possible durable solutions has changed over time, its ability to find solutions for refugee situations appears to be decreasing. In fact, refugees are spending longer periods in exile, and increased attention is now being paid to the rise of protracted refugee situations.[22]

A protracted refugee situation (PRS) is defined by UNHCR as one "in which refugees find themselves in a long-standing and intractable state of limbo" and "their basic rights and essential economic, social and psychological needs remain unfulfilled after years in exile."[23] UNHCR conventionally identifies a major protracted refugee situation as one where more than 25,000 refugees have been in exile for more than five years.[24] However, these criteria are somewhat arbitrary and may ignore smaller residual populations that remain after repatriation, those outside UNHCR's mandate, or changes that arise due to repeat migration. The important point is that PRSs involve refugee populations that are longstanding or recurring. Because refugees may spend significant amounts of time in insecure camp-like situations, their existence often has negative implications for refugees' human rights and states' security. Such situations are the result of a political failure to ensure that refugees have timely access to durable solutions such as repatriation, local integration, or resettlement. Their negative consequences are often exacerbated by the inadequate levels of protection, assistance and social and economic opportunities available to refugees in many developing countries.

PRSs are not new. One of the earliest recognized PRSs was the situation of refugees in Europe after the Second World War, many of whom remained in limbo until the 1960s. During the 1970s and 1980s, refugees were displaced for long periods in Africa, Latin America and South-East Asia. However, many of these situations were not initially perceived as particularly problematic for host states because those displaced by anti-colonial liberation wars in Africa were expected to eventually go home, while those exiled by the Cold War were often welcomed by the West. Furthermore, with the end of the Cold War, the resolution of a number of conflicts allowed significant repatriation to take place by the mid-1990s. During the 1990s, however, a number of intra-state conflicts in states such as Somalia, Sierra Leone, Liberia, Rwanda, and Bosnia led to the creation of a number of new refugee situations. UNHCR's focus during the 1990s was mainly on the provision of assistance in humanitarian emergencies, and it placed less emphasis on enhancing refugee protection or on finding durable solutions other than repatriation once the emergency phase was over. Consequently, many of those refugee situations remained unresolved.[25]

Today, around 6 million refugees are in protracted situations, representing some two-thirds of the world's refugees. What is striking is the fact that refugees are spending longer periods in exile, and that more refugee situations are becoming protracted. In 1993, the average duration of a refugee situation was nine years. By 2004, the average length of exile was an incredible 17 years.[26] There are now more than 30 PRSs around the world (Table 5.1).

In addition, although they fall outside of UNHCR's mandate for historical reasons, there are around 4 million registered Palestinian refugees in longstanding exile in the Middle East.[27]

PRSs originate from the very states that have come to dominate international discussions on "failed and fragile states," such as Afghanistan and Somalia to name but two. While there is increasing recognition that the international community must address the challenges posed by these states, little attention has been paid to the implications of protracted exile. In fact, PRSs are not inevitable, but are the result of a series of impasses. These situations are the combined result of the prevailing conditions in the country of origin, the policy responses of the country of asylum and the lack of sufficient donor engagement. The primary causes of PRSs are to be found in the failure to engage in countries of origin and the failure to consolidate peace agreements. UNHCR has placed greater emphasis on PRSs over the past few years, and it has piloted a range of new approaches to facilitating access to durable solutions. However, the institutional structures for addressing PRSs remain inadequate in terms of their ability to facilitate a greater political commitment by states to ensuring timely access to durable solutions and in terms of ensuring adequate collaboration across the UN system.

The prolonged presence of refugees is frequently perceived by host states as a burden rather than a potential benefit. Rather than trying to use and develop their skills and talents, and integrate them, many states limit refugees' physical mobility and social integration. They are often restricted to camps or confined settlements in isolated, insecure border regions. Developing states generally devolve responsibility for running such camps and settlements to UNHCR as a means of limiting their own financial and political commitments. UNHCR is therefore often drawn into the long-term management of refugee camps, which become quasi-permanent residential structures rather than the instruments of interim protection that they were intended to be.[28]

Such long-term encampment has significant human rights implications. The United States Committee for Refugees and Immigrants

Table 5.1 Major protracted refugee situations as of 1 January 2005

Country of asylum	Origin	End of 2004
Algeria	Western Sahara	165,000
Armenia	Azerbaijan	235,000
Burundi	Dem. Rep. of Congo	48,000
Cameroon	Chad	39,000
China	Viet Nam	299,000
Congo	Dem. Rep. of Congo	59,000
Côte d'Ivoire	Liberia	70,000
Dem. Rep. of Congo	Angola	98,000
Dem. Rep. of Congo	Sudan	45,000
Egypt	Occupied Palestinian Territory	70,000
Ethiopia	Sudan	90,000
Guinea	Liberia	127,000
India	China	94,000
India	Sri Lanka	57,000
Islamic Rep. of Iran	Afghanistan	953,000
Islamic Rep. of Iran	Iraq	93,000
Kenya	Somalia	154,000
Kenya	Sudan	68,000
Nepal	Bhutan	105,000
Pakistan	Afghanistan (UNHCR estimate)	960,000
Rwanda	Dem. Rep. of Congo	45,000
Saudi Arabia	Occupied Palestinian Territory	240,000
Serbia and Montenegro	Bosnia and Herzegovina	95,000
Serbia and Montenegro	Croatia	180,000
Sudan	Eritrea	111,000
Thailand	Myanmar	121,000
Uganda	Sudan	215,000
United Rep. of Tanzania	Burundi	444,000
United Rep. of Tanzania	Dem. Rep. of Congo	153,000
Uzbekistan	Tajikistan	39,000
Yemen	Somalia	64,000
Zambia	Angola	89,000
Zambia	Dem. Rep. of Congo	66,000

Source: UNHCR *The State of the World's Refugees: Human Displacement in the New Millennium* (2006).

(USCRI), for example, launched a campaign in 2004, condemning the practice of what it refers to as the "warehousing" of refugees. It argued that long-term encampment represents "a denial of rights and a waste of humanity" because of the way in which it limits refugees' access to a range of rights. In particular, refugees in PRSs frequently do not receive a number of 1951 Convention rights such as the right to freedom of movement (Article 26) and the right to seek wage-earning employment (Article 17).[29] They also often face a range of other limitations and threats to their security. Idleness, lack of social and educational opportunities, and dependency have been highlighted as contributing to generalized insecurity. With few opportunities, some refugees have turned to a range of negative coping strategies such as crime, drugs or prostitution.[30] Many refugee camps are also extremely insecure. Although the situation has improved, the Dadaab camps in Kenya, for example, have often been associated with arms trafficking, cross-border banditry, sex and gender-based violence, and significant tensions with the local community.[31]

As well as human rights implications, PRSs also have important consequences for security, particularly for host states in the developing world, but also regionally and internationally. As with mass influx situations, PRSs also give rise to a number of direct and indirect security concerns.[32] In particular, refugees emanating from states such as Afghanistan and Somalia have been identified as a potential source of instability for host states because of their possible on-going attachment to armed groups of non-state actors engaged in insurgent or terrorist activities. For such groups, the environment of a PRS, in which there are few economic and social opportunities for young men, may represent a potential source of terrorist recruitment.

Protracted refugee situations also pose an indirect security concern as they may lead to or exacerbate grievances among the local population. The processes of structural adjustment and democratization that have taken place in much of the developing world have increased the scope for such tensions. In Sub-Saharan Africa, for example, large numbers of self-settled rural refugees were present in a number of states during the 1960s and 1970s. Since then, however, structural adjustment processes have led to the reduction of social services available to citizens in many states. With the emergence of democracy in many of these states, it is increasingly difficult for politicians in states such as Tanzania and Kenya to argue that refugees should be entitled to services that are unavailable to citizens.[33] The existence of PRS can also indirectly represent a threat to state security through the impact they may have on inter-communal tensions. Where the long-term presence of refugees from a given racial, ethnic or religious grouping changes the balance of power among different identity groups, it may play a destabilizing role.

The problems associated with PRSs, however, are not confined to the host states in the developing world but have wider implications, both regionally and internationally. If PRSs lead to instability and contribute to on-going conflict or offer a fertile source of recruitment for extremists, this may ultimately have consequences for states beyond the region. Furthermore, the failure to address PRSs appears to have implications for irregular migration from South to North. For example, a UNHCR-commissioned survey on the underlying causes of the irregular secondary movement of Somali refugees highlighted how the absence of durable solutions and effective protection in first countries of asylum was a major motive for onward migratory movements to Europe and elsewhere.[34] In other words, in situations in which refugees are unable to find adequate protection and timely access to durable solutions in their region of origin, they may have to seek these outside of that region.

The politics of durable solutions

The rising significance of PRSs is a clear illustration of the shortcomings of UNHCR's ability to find solutions for refugees. While the search for durable solutions has been a central part of UNHCR's mandate since its inception, the role of the three main durable solutions and the relative priority accorded to each by UNHCR have changed over time. During the Cold War and the anti-colonial liberation struggles of the 1960s and 1970s, those fleeing Communist regimes and colonial oppression were granted refugee status on the assumption that repatriation was not an immediately viable option.[35] Consequently, resettlement and *de facto* local integration were the principal durable solutions until the 1980s.[36] From the end of the Cold War, however, this has changed. Northern states have been increasingly concerned to limit immigration, in general, and asylum in particular, and their commitment to resettlement subsequently diminished to the point of insignificance. Meanwhile, in the context of structural adjustment, democratization and diminishing international assistance, Southern states have become increasingly reluctant to countenance local integration.[37] From the 1990s, repatriation therefore emerged as "the preferred durable solution" of states and UNHCR. The difficulty with this approach, however, was that it led states and UNHCR often to assume that the only feasible option for the provision of durable solution was to wait for a given conflict to end and then to facilitate return. During the 1990s, this position also led UNHCR to attempt repatriation prematurely to countries like Afghanistan, Burma/Myanmar, Burundi and Liberia in ways that proved both dangerous for refugees and unsustainable. In these situations, little was done to ensure that repatriation took place alongside peacebuilding and post-conflict reconstruction and development.

Reflecting the increasingly protracted nature of many refugee situations and the inadequacy of the repatriation attempts of the 1990s,

UNHCR began to develop a range of new ideas relating to durable solutions in recent years.[38] In particular, a core element of the Convention Plus process was to promote greater international burden sharing as a means to enhance refugees' access to durable solutions. In relation to repatriation, UNHCR developed the notion of the 4Rs (repatriation, reintegration, rehabilitation and reconstruction) in order to enhance the sustainability of repatriation. The 4Rs was based on the acknowledgment that return must involve more than transferring refugees across a border; it requires the creation of an environment conducive to return. The key to this was acknowledged to be inter-agency collaboration, particularly with development actors such as the World Bank and UNDP, whose work focuses on post-conflict reconstruction. This approach has recently been applied in post-conflict states such as Afghanistan, Liberia, Sierra Leone, and Sri Lanka.[39]

In relation to local integration, UNHCR conceived the idea of development through local integration (DLI). The approach drew upon the precedents of RAD developed by UNHCR in ICARA I and II and CIREFCA in the 1980s. Its intention was to facilitate permanent integration through providing integrated community development assistance to both refugees and host communities, in ways that could enable the presence of refugees to be perceived as a benefit to local communities and host governments. Given how controversial local integration is for many developing states, UNHCR also conceived the notion of development assistance for refugees (DAR), which was intended to facilitate interim self-reliance for refugees without necessarily leading to permanent integration or citizenship.

In the case of both DLI and DAR, however, UNHCR has been largely unsuccessful in persuading states to adopt such an approach despite the potential of targeted development assistance to address many of the negative consequences of PRSs. Southern states have generally been unwilling to consider either local integration or self-reliance unless it is accompanied by significant additional development assistance. Meanwhile, Northern states have been unwilling to provide the levels of additional development assistance that might entice Southern states to reconsider this position. Consequently, the only two notable examples of DLI and DAR have been in Zambia and Uganda, where, to different degrees, refugees have been given access to freedom of movement, access to land, and livelihood opportunities.[40]

UNHCR has also attempted to revive the practice of resettlement by developing the idea of the "strategic use of resettlement." The concept revolves around the realization that resettlement can play a complementary role in leverage, with improved protection and prospects of solutions for those refugees, not resettlement. Since resettlement represents a tangible mechanism through which states can show solidarity with a country of first asylum, and since resettlement may constitute the only viable durable solution for specific small groups or individual refugees, it is seen to have added strategic utility.[41] In this way, resettlement countries used resettlement strategically during the Indochinese refugee crisis to extract guarantees of temporary asylum from host states in the region, as outlined in Chapter 2. Since its origins in the Convention Plus process, the possible strategic use of resettlement to overcome the impasses inherent in PRSs has been the topic of significant discussions between resettlement countries, NGOs and UNHCR, especially through the Annual Tripartite Consultations on Resettlement.

Historically, one of the most successful ways in which UNHCR has worked to overcome PRSs is through Comprehensive Plans of Action. CPAs represent multilateral approaches to ensure access to durable solutions for refugees within a given regional context. Such approaches can be regarded as CPAs insofar as they were *comprehensive* in terms of drawing on a range of durable solutions; *cooperative* in terms of involving additional burden sharing or responsibility sharing between countries of origin and asylum, and third countries acting as donors or resettlement countries; and *collaborative* in terms of working across UN agencies and with NGOs.[42]

As outlined in Chapter 2, the two most successful precedents for UNHCR-led CPAs were the Indochinese CPA and CIREFCA. Based on the success of these precedents, UNHCR attempted to revive the concept of the CPA in the context of the Convention Plus initiative.[43] It developed the CPA for Somali refugees in 2005, which aimed to draw upon many of the new ideas on durable solutions developed in Convention Plus and apply them to the situation of Somali refugees in Kenya, the Yemen, Djibouti, and Ethiopia. Unfortunately, there was very little political backing for the initiative. One of the reasons for this, aside from the deteriorating security situation in Somalia, was that UNHCR did not adequately learn lessons from what made the earlier precedents so successful. The Somali CPA was conceived with a technocratic logic: it devised programs and projects with the intention of putting them before a donor conference.

In contrast, the Indochinese CPA and CIREFCA were conceived as sustained political processes with ongoing dialogue and negotiation. What enabled international cooperation to take place was that the Office provided clear political leadership. Diplomatically skilled individuals within UNHCR recognized the range of states' interests in the regions and channeled them into a commitment to refugee protection. Of particular importance, the Office recognized that the relevant stakeholders had interests in a range of other issue-areas such as security, migration, trade or development, and persuaded those states that these wider linked interests might be met through a commitment to refugee protection. On a practical level, their success was based upon having country of origin involvement, strong collaboration with other actors and institutions, a strong UNHCR presence in the region, and ownership of the process by the states in the region.

Replicating the success of past CPAs will be an important priority for UNHCR if it is to meet the challenge of finding comprehensive solutions to the world's PRSs. The precedents undoubtedly took place at a very opportune time for international cooperation at the end of the Cold War. Nevertheless, two lessons are clear. UNHCR requires a greater political capacity if it is to successfully use CPAs to overcome longstanding refugee situations. This requires UNHCR to develop the necessary personnel structures and to recruit and promote individuals with the necessary political and analytical skills. The Office also needs to create a permanent political infrastructure within headquarters to take the lead in finding solutions to PRSs. Most importantly, overcoming PRSs cannot be UNHCR's role alone. The causes and consequences of prolonged refugee situations go far beyond the scope of UNHCR mandate. Addressing them relies upon the creation of a UN-wide collaborative institutional framework that would incorporate a role for the Office of the Secretary-General, development agencies such as the World Bank and UNDP, the newly-established UN Peacebuilding Commission, and migration actors.

The future of UNHCR's mandate

The expanded role that UNHCR has taken on IDP protection, the enduring challenge of finding solutions to protracted refugee situations and UNHCR's broader place within the UN system are important parts of a wider debate on the future role of the Office. In particular, they highlight the question of whether UNHCR should be strictly a refugee protection organization or whether it should take on the broader role of being the UN's protection organization. UNHCR has historically taken on a limited *ad hoc* role in providing protection for some groups of non-refugees such as some IDPs and some stateless people. However, under High Commissioner Guterres, this wider role has become formalized to an unprecedented extent. The institutionalization of the organization's responsibility for IDP protection represents a potentially radical shift towards the reinvention of UNHCR as a wider protection organization. In addition to the Office's new responsibilities for IDP protection, it has increasingly taken on a protection role in natural disasters such as the 2004 Indian Ocean tsunami and the 2005 earthquake in Pakistan.

UNHCR has largely come to play this growing role as an *ad hoc* response to new needs. Over time, it has taken on a wider role in response to specific crises and at the request of the General Assembly. There are legitimate reasons for UNHCR taking on this role. Other groups of displaced people are clearly in need of protection; IDPs, stateless people, and growing numbers of environmentally displaced people all require the support of the international community. Indeed, as the UN system is currently conceived, there are few other UN agencies with the expertise and protection capacity to meet the needs of other groups of displaced people. Given UNHCR's protection focus, and the absence of a more coherent wider UN response to the needs of these other groups, it is not surprising that UNHCR has come to serve a stop-gap for meeting the protection needs of these other groups. Furthermore, with declining refugee numbers in the early twenty-first century, and rising numbers of IDPs, UNHCR has faced the dilemma of how to ensure its ongoing relevance to states.

However, institutionalizing a wider protection role for UNHCR, and conceiving it as the UN protection agency, potentially changes the nature of the Office in ways that may have an impact on its ability to fulfill its core refugee protection role. UNHCR is currently unable to meet the needs of the world's refugees, as illustrated by the growing significance of protracted refugee situations. Its funding and organizational constraints, and the inadequacy of the wider UN response to refugees, would seem to suggest that the Office should be focusing on enhancing its refugee protection and solutions roles before it seeks to expand into other areas. With many refugees without access to effective protection or in protracted refugee situations, UNHCR's original mandate remains unfulfilled and poses a great deal of current and future challenges, even without it taking on greater responsibility. Furthermore, broadening UNHCR's mandate potentially has contradictory implications for UNHCR's refugee protection role. This is not only because it enables UNHCR to be used by donors as a tool for containing potential asylum seekers within their country-of-origin, but also because the necessary management and organizational restructuring potentially divert the Office's focus.

An alternative approach to UNHCR becoming the UN's protection agency would be to create a more coherent UN system to ensure that other actors are able to meet the protection needs of non-refugees. If other agencies had the capacity to respond to the protection needs of other categories of displaced people, UNHCR would not have to take on this role as a stop-gap and would be able to focus on its core refugee-specific mandate, rather than expanding its role to incorporate what is a potentially vast range of categories of people with protection needs. In many ways, this dilemma about the Office's future protection role places UNHCR at a crossroads. Whether it chooses to be the UN's refugee agency or the UN's protection agency will have a profound effect on its future work, and its ability to meet the needs of refugees.

6 Conclusion

Towards the future

International news offers us fresh examples of displacement every day. In 2007, for example, a regional refugee crisis spread rapidly across Central Africa involving the mass exodus of refugees from the Darfur region of Western Sudan into Chad, the Central African Republic, and Cameroon. In the Middle East, one of the largest mass displacements of the last half century was affecting Iraq and its neighbors. By mid-2007, over 2.2 million Iraqis had fled war and civil conflict, mainly to Jordan and Syria but also to other countries in the region while 2 million Iraqis were internally displaced. In addition to these well-publicized refugee emergencies, millions more people fled their homes in search of security and safety. Many entered refugee camps or lived on the margins of overcrowded cities in the developing world. Many will remain in these conditions for many years and even decades, trapped in protracted refugee situations.

Refugees are symptomatic of an insecure and uncertain world. No continent is immune from mass displacement. With increased political and economic volatility, continuing local and regional conflicts, and new environmental pressures, states are increasingly concerned about movements of people within and across national borders. In some unstable regions, host governments fear that refugee camps on their territory will serve as bases and sanctuaries for armed groups that are sources of insurgency, resistance and terrorist movements. Refugee crises also can have an impact on local economies and societies. The presence of refugees can sometimes exacerbate previously existing inter-communal tensions in the host country, shift the balance of power between communities, or cause grievances among local populations. Many host governments, in both the North and South, now present refugee populations as security threats to justify restrictive policies that would not otherwise be permissible.

UNHCR's ability to respond to the needs of refugees is greatly constrained by the increasingly restrictive refugee policies adopted by states. The notion that the Office it is a passive mechanism with no independent agenda of its own, however, is not borne out by the empirical evidence of the past five and a half decades. Although UNHCR has limited material capabilities, it has at times influenced the international political agenda and international responses to humanitarian crises through other sorts of power, such as authority and expertise. It has played a role both in framing the importance of refugee issues for states and in initiating discussions about policy proposals in response to humanitarian crises. In this sense, UNHCR has at times been a locus of power within the international political system.

Given the enduring challenge of protecting refugees and finding solutions to their plight, UNHCR remains an indispensable international organization. This final chapter concludes the book in two ways. It sets out a vision for UNHCR's future role in the global refugee regime, outlining the key challenges that it will face and how it can best respond to them. It then ends by assessing the wider implications of the book's analysis of UNHCR for understanding the role of international organizations in global governance.

UNHCR's role in the global refugee regime

Since its inception, UNHCR has been the central organization within the global refugee regime. It has had responsibility for monitoring and supporting states' compliance with the norms, rules and decision-making procedures set out primarily by the 1951 Convention. Yet, in order to fulfill this role, it has had to adapt to changing historical circumstances. As the political context of its work has evolved, so too has the Office's own organizational structure and approach. Often UNHCR's adaptability has been its strength, allowing it to recognize and respond to the opportunities and constraints presented by each historical juncture. As well as evolving in order to meet its mandate, however, the Office has frequently adapted by expanding its mandate of refugee protection and durable solutions to a range of other areas.

Although the gradual expansion of UNHCR's activities has allowed the organization to grow and maintain its relevance to the interests of key donor states, it has increasingly led to an over-expansion of UNHCR's activities, often in potentially contradictory ways. In fact, taking on an expanded role has had potentially negative consequences for protection and solutions. For example, the Office's growing role in humanitarian operations in the 1990s was also often in conflict with its protection role; in situations such as Former Yugoslavia and Zaire it often found itself providing assistance to those responsible for persecution. Meanwhile, UNHCR's expanded role in care and maintenance since the 1980s has sometimes compromised the Office's ability to effectively advocate for durable solutions. So long as UNHCR is the main provider of assistance to refugees in camps, states are able to defer considering longer-term solutions to protracted refugee situations.

These tensions within UNHCR's work have exacerbated an emerging crisis in the organization's core mandate of protection and solutions for refugees. Despite expanding its work, the Office has struggled to ensure that the world's refugees have access to effective protection in accordance with their 1951 Convention rights. States' unpredictable financial contributions and increasingly restrictive responses to refugees on their territories have meant that protection needs have been inadequately met. Meanwhile, the numbers of refugees in protracted refugee situations and the duration of their exile highlight the ongoing need to ensure refugees' timely access to durable solutions. These ongoing challenges further demonstrate the ongoing relevance of UNHCR's core mandate and the need to reinvigorate its focus on its central responsibilities rather than expanding into new and potentially contradictory areas.

While the relevance of UNHCR's core mandate therefore remains as salient as ever, the nature of displacement is fundamentally changing at the start of the twenty-first century. In particular, globalization, the "War on Terror" and the changing nature of conflict represent key challenges for the Office. Growing transboundary interconnectivity has created new opportunities and incentives for international migration. It has brought with it the development of improved transportation and telecommunications, new diaspora networks, the dramatic growth of human trafficking and smuggling, and the aspirations created by an increasingly global media. These trends have contributed to ever-increasing South–North migration since the 1980s. Within this context, asylum is increasingly intertwined with other forms of migration. Meanwhile, those refugees who do not find effective protection within their region of origin may attempt to use common migration channels in order to move to another continent. Asylum seekers and other migrants often use similar migratory routes and both may have a combination of economic and political motives. Complex transit routes have therefore emerged, in which those in need of international protection are often caught up in broader migratory movements. In areas such as many of the routes to Europe across the Mediterranean, this phenomenon of the "asylum–migration nexus" is extremely evident. This change makes UNHCR's work all the more complex, requiring it to find a way to ensure that protection is available within the context of "mixed migratory movements." While recognizing that states may have legitimate reasons to manage migration, UNHCR needs to ensure that refugees do not face *refoulement* as a consequence of states' undifferentiated responses to these movements.

UNHCR's work is also taking place in a changing security environment. The response to the events of 11 September 2001 has reinforced states' concerns with security. This has led to increasingly restrictionist asylum policies, as states have attempted to assert ever greater control over the entry of foreign nationals onto their territory. The recognition that some terror suspects, such as those involved in the London bombings of 7 July 2005, may have used asylum channels to gain entry to the country has contributed to making states ever more reluctant to allow the spontaneous arrival of asylum seekers. The period since 2001 has consequently seen a reassertion of the use of policies such as detention, interdiction, limitations on asylum seekers' right of appeal, and proposals for offshore processing centers in Northern states. Many Southern states, meanwhile, have used the language of Northern states to further justify restrictions of refugees' rights.

While the new security environment has led to greater border control at the domestic level, it has simultaneously stimulated a growing recognition by Northern states of the need for engagement abroad. Northern states have begun to recognize the interdependence of their citizens' security with potential sources of insecurity in the South. The United States and the European Union, in particular, have increasingly recognized that unless potential sources of terror, instability or injustice are addressed at their source, they may spill over in ways that affect their citizens. In the area of forced migration, this has had a number of implications. The recognition that those displaced may constitute a potential source of threat—either as migrants or terrorists—has led to a growing desire by donor states to encourage "protection in the region of origin," whether through IDP protection or enhancing the protection capacities of host states of first asylum. This new emphasis has been motivated by the aim of using it as a substitute for asylum in the North. To a lesser extent, there has also been an acknowledgement that longstanding protracted refugee situations may represent potential sources of terrorist recruitment. For UNHCR, this represents both an opportunity and a constraint. On the one hand, the new security environment creates a potential incentive for donors to commit to enhancing access to protection and solutions for refugees in the South; on the other hand, the new emphasis has led to new restrictions on asylum in both Northern and Southern states.

UNHCR's ability to fulfill its mandate is also related in complex ways to the contemporary nature of conflict. Since the end of the Cold War, the majority of the world's wars have been intra-state conflicts, often with a complex regional dimension. These conflicts have often been ignored by the international community, which has instead left humanitarian agencies such as UNHCR to address the most visible symptoms of those conflicts as a substitute for engaging with their underlying causes. Yet UNHCR's ability to fulfill its mandate is inextricably related to the nature of those conflicts. In an era in which most states of first asylum identify repatriation as the most desirable durable solution, ensuring that there are appropriate conditions for sustainable return is central to the Office's work. Achieving this relies upon conflict resolution, post-conflict reconstruction and development, and sustainable peacebuilding. Where conflict is protracted, and no cessation of violence is immediately possible, UNHCR faces the challenge of thinking creatively about viable alternatives to repatriation. Rather than resorting to long-term encampment, UNHCR needs to develop ways—such as through an integrated development approach that benefits both refugees and host populations—so that self-sufficiency projects or permanent local integration can be made viable and attractive to host states.

In all these contemporary challenges, UNHCR's work is interconnected in complex ways with broader issue-areas such as migration, security, development, and peacebuilding. In order to fulfill its core mandate of achieving protection and solutions for refugees, UNHCR cannot avoid engaging proactively with these areas. However, this is not an argument for UNHCR to infinitely expand its mandate and become a migration organization or a development organization, for example. Rather, it is an argument for a UNHCR that plays a facilitative and catalytic role in mobilizing other actors to fulfill their responsibilities with respect to refugees. In order to fulfill its core mandate, the Office may need to do more by doing less, and become more focused and strategic in the advocacy, coordination and facilitation role that it plays. This vision for a catalytic UNHCR, capable of fulfilling its protection and solutions mandate in the twenty-first century, has two central elements: one focused on the UN system and the other on states.

First, ensuring effective protection and access to solutions for refugees relies upon a UN system-wide approach. Although UNHCR is the principal international organization with responsibility for refugees, the refugee regime itself goes beyond UNHCR. Refugees should not be seen as exclusively UNHCR's responsibility. Rather, development actors, other humanitarian actors, the UN Peacebuilding Commission, and a possible UN migration organization all need to recognize their role in refugee issues. Only with their active collaboration can UNHCR ensure protection for refugees in the context of wider migratory flows or create the conditions required for repatriation, for example. UNHCR therefore needs to develop clearly defined partnerships with these actors and draw upon their expertise. In order for such collaborative agreements to be effective, the Office of the Secretary-General and the General Assembly need to offer leadership to ensure that other agencies are aware of their responsibilities towards refugees and the need to work cooperatively with UNHCR. Within this overall framework, UNHCR would have a crucial role to play in coordinating, facilitating, and advocating for the response of the UN system. Furthermore, this is a role that UNHCR should not be side-tracked from by having to play a permanent stop-gap role in areas that fall outside and potentially contradict its core mandate.

Second, in order to ensure that states contribute to securing protection and solutions, UNHCR needs to become a more politically engaged actor. Being politically engaged does not require the Office to abandon its Statute obligation to being a non-political organization. Rather, it means that UNHCR should be aware of the highly politicized environment within which it works. This environment is largely determined by the interests and capacities of states. The enduring challenge for UNHCR when working with states is to facilitate and encourage international cooperation and burden sharing that is appropriate in scale, scope, and duration in responding to the global refugee problem.

States can engage in two forms of burden sharing. States may engage in financial burden sharing by providing the resources required by UNHCR and host states to ensure effective protection and to find solutions. States may also engage in physical burden sharing by hosting refugees as a country of asylum, by allowing refugees to locally integrate, or by providing a solution to refugees through resettlement. Generally, states have continued to uphold their broad 1951 Convention obligations to provide asylum, albeit often with an increasingly minimalist interpretation of those obligations. In the absence of a clear legal or normative obligation to engage in burden sharing and to support refugees who have not reached a state's own territory, however, states' contributions to burden sharing have been limited and highly selective. Where such contributions have been made, they have rarely been for purely altruistic reasons. Rather, states have historically contributed to UNHCR's annual budget or provided resettlement because they have had a perceived interest in a specific population or situation. Such interests are usually not related to refugee protection *per se*, but rather emerge from linked issue-areas. In the Cold War context, contributions were often motivated by strategic or foreign policy interests. In the post-Cold War era, they are often motivated by concerns with security, migration or development.

To successfully channel states' interests in linked issue-areas into a commitment to refugee protection, UNHCR needs to build on these broader interests of states to encourage action that enhances the protection of refugees and contributes to solutions for their plight. Contemporary challenges such as the asylum-migration nexus and the War on Terror may represent both opportunities and constraints for UNHCR. On the one hand, they create "hooks" that UNHCR can use to appeal to donor states to engage in the need for more effective protection and durable solutions. By persuading Northern states that their wider interests in migration control and security can best be met by enhancing protection capacity in the South or ensuring refugees' timely access to durable solutions, for example, UNHCR may be able to increase levels of burden sharing. Additional financial support and targeted development assistance, might, in turn, persuade and enable Southern host states to enhance the quality of protection that they offer to refugees. On the other hand, however, appealing to these interests also poses risks. In particular, it may reinforce the exclusionary logic that underpins many states' restrictive asylum policies or contribute to undermining the normative basis of the refugee regime.

Whether UNHCR uses issue-linkage to try to channel states' interests in other issue-areas into a commitment to refugee protection, or relies on its moral authority, it is clear that the Office cannot withdraw from recognizing and responding to world politics. Historically, UNHCR has been at its most effective when it has played a politically engaged role. The successes of CIREFCA and the Indochinese CPA, for example, owe a great deal to the political leadership of the Office and its willingness to recognize and engage with states' wider interests. In contrast, UNHCR has historically been at its least effective when it has attempted to take on a passive and technocratic role. The challenge is to appeal to interests and engage with politics without being involuntarily shaped and molded by political circumstances.

Broader insights for global governance

Over recent years greater attention has been paid by academics and policy-makers to what has become known as global governance.

Global governance broadly relates to the way in which a regulatory framework is negotiated, monitored and enforced at the international level. The role of UNHCR in the global refugee regime potentially offers wider insights for global governance. In particular, it contributes to understanding the role of international organizations in upholding an institutional framework designed to regulate the behavior of sovereign states.

UNHCR's position highlights aspects of the challenges faced by an international organization vested with responsibility for upholding a normative framework. It exemplifies the challenges posed by maintaining a normative agenda in the context of a changing international society. UNHCR and the refugee regime were created at a historical juncture when there was scope for negotiating an institutional framework for refugee protection that privileged human rights. While the regime also implicitly focused on ensuring a return to stability in Western Europe in the aftermath of the Second World War, it was also heavily focused on justice. The focus of the refugee convention primarily on refugees' rights highlights this emphasis. The spirit of optimism and humanitarianism that epitomized the immediate aftermath of the late 1940s and early 1950s, and the initial European focus of the regime contributed to the creation of a normative framework focused heavily on justice in terms of human rights, rather than simply security and state sovereignty.

The history of UNHCR is of particular wider interest because it highlights the challenges and pitfalls faced by an organization vested with defending a regime premised on justice, over a period in which states have become far more concerned with order, and in which power and interests have been the dominant influences in world politics. In other words, the refugee regime is one which states would almost certainly not have agreed to at any subsequent historical juncture. It institutionalized the values of a relatively small number of negotiating states at a very specific point in history. This has left UNHCR as the guardian of a set of normative principles which have often been in tension with the changing interests of states. The subsequent emergence of new interests and ideas has placed the Office in a precarious and delicate position *vis-à-vis* those states. On the one hand, the Office has had to try to exert an autonomous influence on states; on the other, it has had to maintain the support of key donor states by meeting their perceived interests.

UNHCR has faced two major structural obstacles in attempting uphold those norms within a changing international society. First, it has been limited in the power it has to influence states. Although it has not been a passive barometer of donor states' interests, the tools it has had to assert its own autonomous agency have been limited. In particular, it has used two principal means: moral authority and normative persuasion, on the one hand, and appealing to the interests of states, on the other hand. These means have often been in tension with one another as appealing to short-term *realpolitik* has not always contributed to underpinning states' normative commitment to refugee protection. Second, UNHCR's responsibility to uphold the refugee regime has occasionally come into conflict with its own organizational interests. As an organization with its own complex internal dynamics, its own interests have not always been the same as those of the constituency it seeks to represent. At times, organizational expansion has been in the interests of the Office's leadership and bureaucracy. However, it has not necessarily served the fulfillment of UNHCR's core mandate or furthered the interests of refugees. In particular, the expansion of the organization during the 1990s into areas such as emergency relief and IDP protection may have brought prestige, additional funding and new jobs, but this might have been in tension with the fulfillment of the Office's core mandate.

In many ways it is these structural challenges that have served to define the historical trajectory of the organization. While seeking to maintain its normative agenda, it has often adapted its own mandate and even compromised the norms underpinning the regime in order to ensure that the regime and the Office's work retain their relevance to states. Ensuring that its work is perceived to meet the perceived interests of key donor states has led to the conception of many new initiatives—some of which have enhanced the credibility of the Office and others of which have served to undermine its moral authority. Similarly, UNHCR's expansion and adaptation have also sometimes been driven by organizational concerns rather than a focus on the core mandate.

UNHCR is a unique international organization, which has adapted and changed over time in order to balance its own organizational interests, the interests of key donors, and the need to uphold its normative agenda. Its precarious place in world politics has made it an international organization that has had to respond to structural opportunities and constraints in order to survive and fulfill its mandate. Yet, it has continued to maintain a significant degree of autonomous agency and the ability to influence states, in spite of its limited power. UNHCR's history provides a story that offers lessons for other global institutions focused on maintaining values of justice and human rights within an international system in which power and interests dominate. In particular, it highlights the significant role that an international organization can play as the guardian of an institutional framework over time in spite of changing configurations of interests and power relations. However, it also highlights how the tensions implicit to this role can shape the trajectory of the regime and the organization itself.

As UNHCR prepares to navigate the challenges of displacement in the twenty-first century, it is important to understand the origins of these tensions, how they have evolved over time, and how the organization has tried to reconcile its mandate with the interests of states. As the results of the past half-century make clear, it is only by learning and responding effectively to these lessons that the organization will be able to realize its mandate of protecting refugees and finding a solution to their plight.

Notes

Foreword

1 David P. Forsythe and Barbara J. Rieffer-Flanagan, *The International Committee of the Red Cross: A Neutral Humanitarian Actor* (London: Routledge, 2006).

2 David Korn and Thomas G. Weiss, *Internal Displacement: Conceptualization and its Consequences* (London: Routledge, 2006); Julie A. Mertus, *The United Nations and Human Rights: A Guide for a New Era* (London: Routledge, 2005); Bertrand G. Ramcharan, *Contemporary Human Rights Ideas* (London: Routledge, 2008).

3 Sadako Ogata, *The Turbulent Decade: Confronting the Refugee Crises of the 1990s* (New York: W. W. Norton, 2005), 25.

4 Gil Loescher, *The UNHCR and World Politics: A Perilous Path* (Oxford: Oxford University Press, 2001) and *Beyond Charity: International Cooperation and the Global Refugee Problem* (Oxford: Oxford University Press, 1993).

5 UNHCR, *The State of the World's Refugees* has been published by Oxford University Press in 1993, 1995, 1997, 2000, 2006, each with a different sub-title.

6 Alexander Betts and Jean-François Durieux, "Convention Plus as a Norm-Setting Exercise," *Journal of Refugee Studies* 20, no. 3 (2007): 509–535; Alexander Betts, "North-South Cooperation in the Global Refugee Regime: The Role of Linkages," *Global Governance*, 14, no. 2 (April 2008); Alexander Betts, "Comprehensive Plans of Action: Insights from CIREFCA and the Indochinese CPA," New Issues in Refugee Research, Working Paper No. 120 (Geneva: UNHCR, 2006); Alexander Betts, "Rethinking Durable Solutions," in *The State of the World's Refugees: Human Displacement in the New Millennium,* ed. Nada Merheb (Oxford: Oxford University Press, 2006), 128–144.

7 Gil Loescher and James Milner, "Protracted Refugee Situations: Domestic and International Security Implications," Adelphi Paper No. 375 (Oxford: Oxford University Press, 2005); Gil Loescher and James Milner, "The Missing Link: The Need for Comprehensive Engagement in Regions of Refugee Origin," *International Affairs* 79, no. 3 (May 2003): 595–617; Gil Loescher and James Milner, "The Long Road Home: Protracted Refugee Situations in Africa," *Survival* 47, no. 2 (2005): 153–174; Gil Loescher, James Milner, Edward Newman, and Gary Troeller, "Protracted Refugee

Situations and the Regional Dynamics of Peacebuilding," *Conflict, Security & Development* 7, no. 3 (2007): 491–501.

Introduction

1 For further development of these arguments, see Gil Loescher, *The UNHCR and World Politics: A Perilous Path* (Oxford: Oxford University Press, 2001).

1 The origins of international concern for refugees

1 For an analysis of the treatment of refugees by states before the twentieth century, see Phil Orchard, "It's Always Darkest Before the Dawn: Displacement, Institutional Development and the Normative Environment. The Case of the League of Nations and the United Nations," paper presented at international conference on refugees and international law, Oxford, 15–16 December 2006, and B. Porter, *The Refugee Question in Mid-Victorian Politics* (Cambridge: Cambridge University Press, 1970).
2 Claudena Skran, *Refugees in Inter-war Europe: The Emergence of a Regime* (Oxford: Clarendon Press, 1995).
3 For the background, see Kim Salomon, *Refugees in the Cold War: Toward a New International Refugee Regime in the Early Postwar Era* (Lund: Lund University Press, 1991); Guy Goodwin-Gill, *The Refugee in International Law* (Oxford: Clarendon Press, 1996); James Hathaway, *The Law of Refugee Status* (Toronto: Butterworths, 1991).
4 In fact, it was not until the 1951 Convention that the refugee definition was expanded to include a group dimension by including "membership in a particular social group" as a basis for a well-founded fear of persecution.
5 See Goodwin-Gill, *The Refugee in International Law.*
6 Michael Barnett and Martha Finnemore, *Rules for the World: International Organizations in Global Politics* (Ithaca, NY: Cornell University Press, 2004).

2 UNHCR in the Cold War, 1950–1991

1 Paragraph 2 of UNHCR's 1950 Statute states: "the work of the High Commissioner shall be of an entirely non-political character; it shall be humanitarian and social and shall relate, as a rule, to groups and categories of refugees."
2 UNHCR, *The State of the World's Refugees: In Search of Solutions* (Oxford: Oxford University Press, 1995).
3 The history of UNHCR during the Cold War draws upon Gil Loescher, *The UNHCR and World Politics: A Perilous Path* (Oxford: Oxford University Press, 2001). See also Louise Holborn, *Refugees: A Problem of Our Time*, 2 vols (Methuen, NJ: Scarecrow Press, 1975) and UNHCR, *The State of the World's Refugees: Fifty Years of Humanitarian Action* (Oxford: Oxford University Press, 2000).
4 Gil Loescher and John Scanlan, *Calculated Kindness: Refugees and America's Half-Open Door* (New York: Free Press, 1986).
5 Gil Loescher, *Beyond Charity: International Cooperation and the Global Refugee Crisis* (New York: Oxford University Press, 1989).

6 Loescher, *UNHCR and World Politics.*

7 For background to UNHCR's role in the Algerian refugee crisis, see Cecilia Ruthstrom-Ruin, *Beyond Europe* (Lund: Lund University Press, 1993).

8 Interview with Bernard Alexander who was UNHCR's chief of cabinet at the time, Oxford, 1986.

9 Interview with Auguste Lindt, UNHCR Oral History Project.

10 Ibid.

11 For background, see Aristide Zolberg, Astri Suhrke and Serio Aguayo, *Escape from Violence: Conflict and the Refugee Crisis in the Developing World* (New York: Oxford University Press, 1989).

12 Gil Loescher, "Refugee Movements and International Security," Adelphi Paper (London: International Institute for Strategic Studies, 1992).

13 In a press release on the day he took office, Schnyder noted "a shift in emphasis to groups in other continents" and stated that "in his opinion the 'good offices' concept was elastic enough to permit him, when asked, to bring effective aid to nearly any group of refugees provided there was sufficient interest and support on the part of the international community." UNHCR press release, N. Ref. 638, Geneva, 1 February 1961.

14 Felix Schnyder, "Les aspects juridiques actues du problème des refugiés," *Recueil*, 114 (Leiden : Academie de Droit International, 1965).

15 Interview with Felix Schnyder, Locarno, Switzerland, 1988.

16 Organization of African Unity, "The Organization of African Unity Convention Governing Specific Aspects of Refugee Problems in Africa", OAU Document CM/267/Rev.1 (10 September 1969).

17 UNHCR, *The Cartagena Declaration of 1984* (Geneva: UNHCR, 1985).

18 Sadruddin Aga Khan, *Legal Problems Related to Refugees and Displaced Persons* (The Hague: Academy of International Law, 1976).

19 See Zolberg *et al.*, *Escape from Violence.*

20 For a discussion of the significance of "refugee warriors" during this period, see Zolberg *et al.*, *Escape from Violence*, Loescher, *Refugee Movements and International Security.*

21 *World Refugee Survey* (Washington, D.C.: US Committee for Refugees, 1989).

22 These views were expressed in Jean-Pierre Hocké, "Beyond Humanitarianism: The Need for Political Will to Resolve Today's Refugee Problem," in *Refugees and International Relations*, eds Gil Loescher and Laila Monahan (Oxford: Oxford University Press, 1989), 37–48. See also Lawyers' Committee for Human Rights, *UNHCR at 40: Refugee Protection at the Crossroads* (New York: Lawyers' Committee for Human Rights, 1990).

23 UNHCR, "Note on International Protection," (Geneva: UNHCR, July 15, 1986).

24 UN General Assembly resolution 35/42 of 25 November 1980.

25 This total was roughly half the amount requested by African states. The largest contributions were received from: USA ($285 million), European Economic Community ($68 million), West Germany ($34 million), and Japan ($33 million). See Barry N. Stein, "ICARA II: Burden Sharing and Durable Solutions," in *Refugees: A Third World Dilemma*, ed. John R. Rogge (Totowa, NJ: Rowman and Littlefield, 1987).

26 UNHCR Archives, "Lesotho Government Assistance Proposals For Submission to the Conference," 19/12/80 (Fonds UNHCR 11, 391.62/113).

27 UN General Assembly resolution 37/197 of 18 December 1982.
28 Operational paragraph 5, UN General Assembly resolution 37/197 of 18 December 1982.
29 Robert F. Gorman, *Coping with Africa's Refugee Burden: A Time for Solutions* (The Hague: Martinus Nijhoff, 1989).
30 Ibid.: 36–40.
31 CIREFCA represents the acronym for the Spanish title of the conference, *La Conferencia Internacional sobre los Refugiados Centroamericanos.*
32 For a detailed analysis, see Alexander Betts, "Comprehensive Plans of Action: Insights from CIREFCA and the Indo-Chinese CPA," *New Issues in Refugee Research*, Working Paper No. 120 (Geneva: UNHCR, 2006).
33 UNHCR Archives, "International Conference on Central American Refugees, Guatemala City, May 1989: Preliminary Information," memo, Mr Deljoo to Mr Asomani, 5/12/88 (UNHCR Fonds 11, Series 3, 391.86, HCR/NYC/1466).
34 UNHCR, "Review of the CIREFCA Process," (1994), available at: www.unhcr.ch
35 UNHCR, *State of the World's Refugees: Fifty Years of Humanitarian Action* (Oxford: Oxford University Press, 2000), 84.
36 *New York Times*, "Vietnam and Laos Finally Join Talks on Refugees," 30 October 1988.
37 UNHCR Archives, memo, Sergio Vieira de Mello to Refeeudin Ahmed, Secretary-General's Office, "Recommended Opening Speech for Kuala Lumpur Meeting, 7–9 March", 22/2/89 (UNHCR Fonds 11, Series 3, 391.89 HCR/NYC/0248).
38 *New York Times*, "Vietnam and Laos Finally Join Talks on Refugees."
39 Pierre Jambor, the UNHCR Representative to Thailand, had first suggested using screening in a note as early as 1986 and developed the ideas through a Ford Foundation-funded study on the Indochinese. Although the idea was initially met with resistance in UNHCR's Department of Refugee Law and Doctrine, it gradually gained support.
40 For details of the CPA, see Courtland Robinson, *Terms of Refuge: The Indochinese Exodus and the International Response* (London: Zed Books, 1989): 187–230; Courtland Robinson, "The Comprehensive Plan of Action for Indochinese Refugees, 1989–1997: Sharing the Burden and Passing the Buck," *Journal of Refugee Studies*, 17, no. 3 (2004): 319–333; Shamsul Bronee, "The History of the Comprehensive Plan of Action," *International Journal of Refugee Law*, 4, no. 4 (1992): 534–559.

3 UNHCR in the post-Cold War era

1 The following draws from Gil Loescher, *The UNHCR and World Politics: A Perilous Path* (Oxford: Oxford University Press, 2001). See also Michael Barnett and Martha Finnemore, *Rules for the World: International Organizations in Global Politics* (Ithaca, NY: Cornell University Press, 2004).
2 UHNCR, *The State of the World's Refugees: A Humanitarian Agenda* (Oxford: Oxford University Press, 1997), 143.
3 Michael Barnett makes this point in "Humanitarian with a Sovereign Face: UNHCR in the Global Undertow," *International Migration Review*, 35, no. 1 (2001): 244–277.

4 In 1992, UNHCR noted:

> Criteria for promotion and organization of large scale repatriation must balance protection needs of the refugees against the political imperative towards resolving refugee problems ... the realization of a solution in a growing number of refugee situations today is most likely when the solution is made an integral part of a "package" which strikes a humane balance between the interests of affected states and the legal rights, as well as humanitarian needs, of the individuals concerned.
>
> (UNHCR, *Note on International Protection*, UN doc. A/AC.96/799 (1992), paras 38 and 39)

5 UNHCR, "Bridging the Gap Between Returnee Aid and Development: A Challenge for the International Community" (Geneva: UNHCR, 1992).
6 Several of the major emergencies are dealt with in Sadako Ogata, *The Turbulent Decade: Confronting the Refugee Crises of the 1990s* (New York: W.W. Norton, 2005). See also UNHCR, *The State of the World's Refugees: Fifty Years of Humanitarian Action* (Oxford: Oxford University Press, 2000).
7 For a detailed overview of refugee movements during the 1990s, see UNHCR, *State of the World's Refugees: Fifty Years of Humanitarian Action* (Oxford: Oxford University Press, 2000) and Loescher, *The UNHCR and World Politics*.
8 Thomas Weiss and David Korn, *Internal Displacement: Conceptualization and Its Consequences* (London: Routledge, 2006).
9 Report of the Representative of the Secretary-General on Internally Displaced Persons. Submitted Pursuant to Commission on Human Rights Resolution 2002/56, 21 January 2003.
10 Thomas G. Weiss and Leon Gordenker, *NGOs, the UN, and Global Governance* (Boulder, CO: Lynne Rienner, 1996).
11 UN Security Council, "Statement by the President of the Security Council," S/PRST/1992/5, 31 January 1992.
12 See Gil Loescher, *Refugee Movements and International Security*, and Myron Weiner (ed.), *International Migration and Security* (Boulder, CO: Westview Press, 1993).
13 Adam Roberts, "Humanitarian Action in War," Adelphi Paper 305 (London: International Institute of Strategic Studies, 1996).
14 Roberta Cohen and Francis Deng, *Masses in Flight: The Global Crisis of Internal Displacement* (Washington, D.C.: The Brookings Institution, 1998).
15 See Alan Dowty and Gil Loescher, "Refugee Flows as Grounds for International Action," *International Security*, 21, no. 1 (1996: 43–71.
16 Anne Hammerstad, "Refugee Protection and the Evolution of a Security Discourse: The UNHCR in the 1990s," DPhil dissertation, University of Oxford.
17 Ogata, *The Turbulent Decade*.
18 UHNCR, *The State of the World's Refugees: A Humanitarian Agenda* (Oxford: Oxford University Press, 1997).
19 Kofi Annan. *Preventing War and Disaster: A Growing Global Challenge* (New York: UN, 1999), 21.

20 Thomas Weiss, *Humanitarian Intervention* (Cambridge: Polity Press, 2007) and Nicholas Wheeler, *Saving Strangers: Humanitarian Intervention in International Society* (Oxford: Oxford University Press, 2000).
21 Sadako Ogata, "Humanitarian Action: Charity or Realpolitik?" speech, Oslo, 21 October 1997.
22 Hammerstad, "Refugee Protection."
23 United Nations Development Programme (UNDP), *Human Development Report 1994* (New York: Oxford University Press, 1994).
24 UNHCR, *The State of the World's Refugees: A Humanitarian Agenda*; Sadako Ogata, *Peace, Security and Humanitarian Action* (London: IISS, 3 April 1997); Sadako Ogata, "Human Security: A Refugee Perspective," speech, Bergen, 19 May 1999.
25 Hammerstad, "Refugee Protection."
26 Karen Jacobsen and Jeff Crisp, "Introduction: Security in Refugee Populated Areas," *Refugee Survey Quarterly*, 19, no. 1 (2000): 1–2.
27 UN Security Council resolution 1208, 1998.
28 UN Security Council resolution 1296, *Statement of the President of the Security Council*, UN Doc. S/PRST/1992/5, 21 January 1992.
29 UN Security Council, *Report of the Secretary-General on the Protection of Civilians in Armed Conflict*, UN Doc S2001/331, 2001.
30 UNHCR ExCom 1999; UNHCR ExCom 2000.
31 The "safe third country" concept has been increasingly used by states to justify deporting asylum seekers. It is generally used to indicate a country through which an asylum seeker has passed and could have claimed asylum but did not.
32 See US Committee for Refugees (USCR), *Sea Change: Australia's New Approach to Asylum Seekers*, February 2002, www.refugees.org.
33 UNHCR, Convention Plus/Forum Briefing, 7 March 2003, Internal Summary by the Department of International Protection.
34 Erika Feller, "Introduction: Protection Policy in the Making: Third Track of the Global Consultations", *Refugee Survey Quarterly*, 22, no. 2/3 (2003): 1.
35 Declaration of States Parties to the 1951 Convention and or its 1967 Protocol relating to the Status of Refugees", Geneva, 13 December 2001, HCR/MMSP/2001/09.
36 General Assembly resolution 57/187, "Office of the United Nations High Commissioner for Refugees," 18 December 2002.
37 Erika Feller, Volker Türk, and Frances Nicholson (eds), *Refugee Protection in International Law: UNHCR's Global Consultations on International Protection* (Cambridge: Cambridge University Press, 2003).
38 UNHCR, "Convention Plus: At a Glance" (2005), www.unhcr.ch
39 A "first country of asylum" is generally used to designate the first state that an asylum seeker reaches after leaving his or her country of origin and receives formal, legal status as a refugee.
40 UNHCR, "For Durable Solutions for Refugees and Persons of Concern" (Geneva: UNHCR, 2003).
41 UNHCR, *Multilateral Framework of Understandings on Resettlement*, FORUM/2004/6, 16/9/04, www.unhcr.ch
42 See Gil Loescher and James Milner, "The Long Road Home: Protracted Refugee Situations in Africa," *Survival*, 47, no. 2 (2005): 153–174.

43 See BBC News on-line, "Lubbers Quits over UN Sex Claims," 20 February 2005, news.bbc.co.uk/2/hi/europe/4282333.stm
44 UNHCR, *The State of the World's Refugees: Human Displacement in the New Millennium* (Oxford: Oxford University Press, 2006), 14.
45 The "responsibility to protect" sets out the legal and ethical basis for humanitarian intervention. It argues that sovereign states have primary responsibility for the protection of their own citizens but, where they are unable or unwilling to do so, responsibility must be borne by the international community. The report was initially prepared by the International Commission on Intervention and State Sovereignty, convened by the Canadian Government, in 2001 but was adopted as part of the UN reform document in September 2005. See ICISS, *The Responsibility to Protect* (Ottawa: International Development Research Centre, 2001).
46 UNHCR, "UNHCR's Role in Support of an Enhanced Humanitarian Response to Situations of Internal Displacement: Update on UNHCR's Leadership Role within the Cluster Approach and IDP Operational Work Plans," informal consultative meeting, 25 May 2007.
47 UNHCR, "Protracted Refugee Situations," Standing Committee, UN Doc. EC/54/SC/CRP. 14, 10 June 2004.
48 See Gil Loescher, James Milner, Edward Newman, and Gary Troeller (eds), *Protracted Refugee Situations: Politics, Human Rights and Security Implications* (Tokyo: UN University Press, 2008).
49 See Michael Barutciski, "A Critical View on UNHCR's Mandate Dilemmas," *International Journal of Refugee Law*, 14, no. 2/3 (2002): 365–381.

4 UNHCR as a global institution

1 General Assembly Resolution 428 (V), 14 December 1950, Annex, *Statue of the Office of the United Nations High Commissioner for Refugees*, Chapter 1, paragraph 1.
2 General Assembly Resolution 58/153, "Implementing Actions Proposed by the United Nations High Commissioner for Refugees to Strengthen the Capacity of his Office to Carry out its Mandate," 22 December 2003.
3 Gil Loescher, James Milner, Edward Newman and Gary Troeller, "Protracted Refugee Situations and the Regional Dynamics of Peacebuilding", *Conflict, Security and Development*, 7, no. 3 (2007: 491–501).
4 For example, see General Assembly Resolution 61/136, "Enlargement of the Executive Committee of the Programme of the United Nations High Commissioner for Refugees," 19 December 2006.
5 General Assembly Resolution 1166 (XII), "International Assistance to Refugees within the Mandate of the United Nations High Commissioner for Refugees," 26 November 1957.
6 UNHCR, "Executive Committee Membership," www.unhcr.org/excom/40111aab4.html
7 General Assembly Resolution 1166 (XII), "International Assistance to Refugees within the Mandate of the United Nations High Commissioner for Refugees," 26 November 1957.
8 See US Committee for Refugees and Immigrants, *World Refugee Survey 2006* (Washington, D.C./: USCRI, 2006).

9 See Gil Loescher, *The UNHCR and World Politics* (Oxford: Oxford University Press, 2001), 311–312.
10 See UNHCR, *UNHCR Manual*, "Chapter 2: Organizational Structure and Responsibilities" (Geneva: UNHCR, 2004).
11 For a more detailed consideration of UNHCR's organizational culture, see Loescher, *The UNHCR and World Politics,* Chapter 10.
12 UNHCR, Evaluation and Policy Analysis Unit, "The State of UNHCR's Organizational Culture," (Geneva: UNHCR, May 2006), EPAU/2005/08.
13 Details of this section are drawn from UNHCR, "UNHCR, the UN System and other International Organizations," www.unhcr.org/partners/3ba8a28ca.html
14 Javier Blas and Jenny Wiggins, "UN Food Programme Claims It Cannot Afford to Feed the Hungry," *Financial Times*, 16 July 2007.
15 UNHCR, "Promoting Development," in *The State of the World's Refugees: In Search of Solutions* (Oxford: Oxford University Press, 1995).
16 David Forsythe and Barbara Ann Rieffer-Flanagan, *The International Committee of the Red Cross: A Neutral Humanitarian Actor* (London: Routledge, 2007).
17 Van Heuven Goedhart, UN High Commissioner for Refugees, 1953, in UNHCR, "NGO Partnerships in Refugee Protection" (Geneva: UNHCR, 2004), 4.
18 UNHCR, "NGO Partnership in Refugee Protection" (Geneva: UNHCR, 2004), 13.
19 Ibid.: 13.
20 UNHCR, *2006 UNHCR Global Report: Challenges and Achievements* (Geneva: UNHCR, 2007), 46.
21 See Elizabeth G. Ferris, "The Role of Non-Governmental Organizations in the International Refugee Regime," in *Problems of Protection: The UNHCR, Refugees and Human Rights*, eds Niklaus Steiner, Mark Gibney and Gil Loescher (London: Routledge, 2003).
22 Chapter III (20), 1950 Statute of the Office of the High Commissioner for Refugees, Annex to UN General Assembly resolution 428/5, 14 December 1950.
23 Global Policy Forum, "UNHCR: Top Ten Donors 1974–2005," www.global policy.org
24 UNHCR, "Earmarking Patterns in 2006" (Geneva: UNHCR, 2007).
25 Ravi Kanbur *et al.*, *The Future of Development Assistance* (Washington DC: Overseas Development Council, 1999).
26 Alexander Betts, "Public Goods Theory and the Provision of Refugee Protection: The Role of the Joint Product Model in Burden-Sharing Theory," *Journal of Refugee Studies*, 16, no. 3 (2003): 290–1.
27 Niklaus Steiner, "Arguing about Asylum: The Complexity of Refugee Debates in Europe," *New Issues in Refugee Research*, Working Paper No. 48 (Geneva: UNHCR, 2000); Eiko Thielemann "Between Interests and Norms: Explaining Burden-Sharing in the European Union," *Journal of Refugee Studies*, 16, no. 3 (2003): 253–273.
28 Betts, "Public Goods Theory and the Provision of Refugee Protection."
29 Alexander Betts, "North-South Cooperation in the Global Refugee Regime: The Role of Linkages," *Global Governance*, 14, no. 2 (2008). See also Ian Smillie and Larry Minear, *The Quality of Money: Donor Behaviour in Humanitarian Financing* (Sommerville, MA: Humanitarianism and

War Project, The Feinstein International Famine Centre, Tufts University, 2003).

30 Astri Suhrke, "Burden-Sharing During Refugee Emergencies: The Logic of Collective versus National Action," *Journal of Refugee Studies*, 11 no. 4 (1998): 396–415.

31 Gil Loescher and John Scanlan, *Calculated Kindness: Refugees and America's Half-Open Door* (New York: Free Press, 1986).

32 Loescher, *The UNHCR and World Politics*.

33 Alexander Betts and Jean-Francois Durieux, "Convention Plus as a Norm-Setting Exercise," *Journal of Refugee Studies*, 20, no. 3 (2007).

34 See, for example, David Levy and Peter Newell (eds), *The Business of Global Environmental Governance* (Cambridge, MA: MIT Press, 2005); Susan Sell, *Private Power, Public Law: The Globalization of Intellectual Property Rights* (Cambridge: Cambridge University Press, 2003).

5 Protection, solutions, and UNHCR's core mandate

1 General Assembly Resolution 428 (V), 14 December 1950, Annex, *Statue of the Office of the United Nations High Commissioner for Refugees*, Chapter 1, paragraph 1.

2 For more details on the cessation and exclusion clauses, see Guy Goodwin-Gill, *The Refugee in International Law* (Oxford: Clarendon Press, 1996); and UNHCR, *Handbook on Procedures and Criteria for Determining Refugee Status under the 1951 Convention and the 1967 Protocol Relating to the Status of Refugees* (Geneva: UNHCR, 1992).

3 See Aristide Zolberg, Astri Suhrke and Serio Aguayo, *Escape from Violence: Conflict and the Refugee Crisis in the Developing World* (New York: Oxford University Press, 1989).

4 UNHCR, "States Parties to the 1951 Convention Relating to the Status of Refugees and the 1967 Protocol", www.unhcr.org/protect/PROTECTION/3b73b0d63.pdf

5 Andrew Shacknove, "From Asylum to Containment," *International Journal of Refugee Law*, 5, no. 4 (1993): 516–533.

6 Matthew J. Gibney, "The State of Asylum: Democratization, Judicialization and Evolution of Refugee Policy," *New Issues in Refugee Research*, Working Paper No. 50 (Geneva: UNHCR, 2001), 3.

7 For a consideration of these proposals, see Gil Loescher and James Milner, "The Missing Link: The Need for Comprehensive Engagement in Regions of Refugee Origin," *International Affairs*, 79, no. 3 (2003): 595–617.

8 Erika Feller, Volker Türk, and Frances Nicholson (eds), *Refugee Protection in International Law: UNHCR's Global Consultations on International Protection* (Cambridge: Cambridge University Press, 2003), 668–671.

9 UNHCR, *The State of the World's Refugees: Human Displacement in the New Millennium* (Oxford: Oxford University Press, 2006), 159.

10 OHCHR, *The Guiding Principles on Internal Displacement*, E/CN.4/1998/53/Add.2, 11 February 1998, www.unhcr.ch/html/menu2/7/b/principles.htm

11 Vanessa Mattar and Paul White, *Consistent and Predictable Responses to IDPs: A Review of UNHCR's Decision-Making Process*, EPAU/2005/2 (Geneva: UNHCR, 2005).

12 Catherine Phuong, *The International Protection of Internally Displaced Persons* (Cambridge: Cambridge University Press), 82–83.
13 Thomas G. Weiss and David A. Korn, *Internal Displacement: Conceptualization and its Consequences* (Oxford: Routledge, 2006), 71–88.
14 Simon Bagshaw, *Developing a Normative Framework for the Protection of Internally Displaced Persons* (New York: Transnational, 2005), 71–97.
15 Roberta Cohen, "Recent Trends in Protection and Assistance for Internally Displaced People," in *Internally Displaced People: Global Survey* (London: Earthscan, 1998), 4–5.
16 OCHA, *No Refuge: The Challenge of Internal Displacement* (Geneva: OCHA, 2003), Chapter 2.
17 UNHCR, *The State of the World's Refugees: Human Displacement in the New Millennium* (Oxford: Oxford University Press, 2006), 168.
18 Roberta Cohen, "Strengthening Protection of IDPs: The UN's Role," *Georgetown Journal of International Affairs*, Winter (2006): 105.
19 Guy Goodwin-Gill, "Refugee Identity and Protection's Fading Prospect," in *Refugee Rights and Realities*, eds Frances Nicholson and Patrick Twomey (Cambridge: Cambridge University Press, 1999), 246; Guy Goodwin-Gill, "UNHCR and Internal Displacement: Stepping into a Legal and Political Minefield," *World Refugee Survey 2000*, 26–31.
20 Cecile Dubernet, *The International Containment of Displaced Persons: Humanitarian Spaces Without Exit* (Aldershot: Ashgate, 2001); Karin Landgren, "Safety Zones and International Protection: A Dark Grey Area," *International Journal of Refugee Law*, 7 (1995): 436.
21 Michael Barutciski, "The Reinforcement of Non-Admission Policies and the Subversion of UNHCR: Displacement and Internal Assistance in Bosnia-Herzegovina, 1992–1994," *International Journal of Refugee Law*, 8, no. 1/2 (1996): 49–110.
22 See Gil Loescher, James Milner, Edward Newman and Gary Troeller (eds), *Protracted Refugee Situations*.
23 UNHCR, "Protracted Refugee Situations," Standing Committee, 30th Meeting, UN Doc. EC/54/SC/CRP.14, 10 June 2004.
24 Ibid.
25 UNHCR, *The State of the World's Refugees: Human Displacement in the New Millennium*: 108–109.
26 Table 5.1 refers to refugee situations where the number of refugees of a certain origin within a particular country of asylum has been 25,000 or more for at least five consecutive years. Industrialized countries are not included. Data do not include Palestinian refugees under the mandate of the UN Relief and Works Agency for Palestine Refugees in the Near East (UNRWA). Source: UNHCR, *The State of the World's Refugees: Human Displacement in the New Millennium* (Oxford: Oxford University Press, 2006), 107.
27 Gil Loescher and James Milner. *Protracted Refugee Situations: Domestic and International Security Implications*, Adelphi Paper no. 375 (London: Routledge, 2005), 16–17.
28 For analysis of the pros and cons of using camps, see Jeff Crisp and Karen Jacobsen, "Refugee Camps Reconsidered," *Forced Migration Review*, 3 (1998): 27–30; Barbara Harrell-Bond, "Camps: Literature Review," *Forced Migration Review*, 2 (1998): 22–24; Jennifer Hyndman, *Managing Displacement:*

Refugees and the Politics of Humanitarianism (Minnesota: University of Minnesota Press, 2000); Anna Schmidt, "Camps Versus Settlements", *Forced Migration Online Thematic Guides*, www.forcedmigration.org

29 Merrill Smith, "Warehousing Refugees: A Denial of Rights, a Waste of Humanity," *World Refugee Survey* (2004): 40–1.

30 Jeff Crisp, "No Solutions in Sight? The Problem of Protracted Refugee Situations in Africa," *New Issues in Refugee Research*, Working Paper No. 75 (Geneva: UNHCR, 2003).

31 Arthur Helton, *The Price of Indifference* (Oxford: Oxford University Press, 2002), 154–162.

32 James Milner, "Sharing the Security Burden: Towards the Convergence of Refugee Protection and State Security," *Refugee Studies Centre* Working Paper No. 4 (2000).

33 James Milner, *Refugees, the State and the Politics of Asylum in Africa* (Basingstoke: Palgrave Macmillan, 2008).

34 Swiss Forum for Migration, *Movements of Somali Refugees and Asylum Seekers and States' Responses Thereto* (Neuchatel: SFM, 2005).

35 UNHCR, *The State of the World's Refugees: Human Displacement in the New Millennium*: 129

36 B. S. Chimni, "From Resettlement to Involuntary Repatriation: Towards a Critical History of Durable Solutions to Refugee Problems," *New Issues in Refugee Research*, Working Paper No. 2 (Geneva: UNHCR, 1999).

37 Karen Jacobsen, "The Forgotten Solution: Local Integration for Refugees in Developing Countries," *New Issues in Refugee Research*, Working Paper No. 45 (Geneva: UNHCR, 2001).

38 UNHCR, "Framework for Durable Solutions and Persons of Concern" (Geneva: UNHCR, 2003).

39 Betsy Lippman, "The 4Rs: The Way Ahead?" *Forced Migration Review*, 21 (2004): 9–11.

40 Alexander Betts, "International Cooperation and the Targeting of Development Assistance for Refugee Solutions: Lessons from the 1980s," *New Issues in Refugee Research*, Working Paper No. 107 (Geneva: UNHCR, 2004).

41 UNHCR, *The State of the World's Refugees: Human Displacement in the New Millennium*: 142–143.

42 Alexander Betts, "Comprehensive Plans of Action: Insights from CIREFCA and the Indochinese CPA," *New Issues in Refugee Research*, Working Paper No. 125 (Geneva: UNHCR, 2006).

43 UNHCR, "Making Comprehensive Approaches to Resolve Problems More Systematically," 3rd Convention Plus Forum, FORUM/2004/7, 16/9/04.

Select bibliography

Michael Barnett and Martha Finnemore, *Rules for the World: International Organizations in Global Politics* (Ithaca, NY: Cornell University Press, 2004).

Alexander Betts, "North-South Cooperation in the Global Refugee Regime: The Role of Linkages," *Global Governance*, 14, no. 2 (2008).

B. S. Chimni, "From Resettlement to Involuntary Repatriation: Towards a Critical History of Durable Solutions to Refugee Problems," *New Issues in Refugee Research,* Working Paper No. 2 (Geneva: UNHCR, 1999).

Erika Feller, Volker Türk and Frances Nicholson (eds), *Refugee Protection in International Law: UNHCR's Global Consultations on International Protection* (Cambridge: Cambridge University Press, 2003).

Guy Goodwin-Gill and Jane McAdam, *The Refugee in International Law* (Oxford: Oxford University Press, 2007).

Arthur Helton, *The Price of Indifference: Refugees and Humanitarian Action in the New Century* (Oxford: Oxford University Press, 2002).

Louise Holborn, *Refugees: A Problem of Our Time* (Methuen, NJ: Scarecrow Press, 1975).

Gil Loescher, *The UNHCR and World Politics: A Perilous Path* (Oxford: Oxford University Press, 2001).

Gil Loescher, James Milner, Edward Newman and Gary Troeller (eds), *Protracted Refugee Situations: Political, Security and Human Rights Implications* (Tokyo: UN University Press, 2008).

James Milner, *Refugees, the State and the Politics of Asylum in Africa* (Basingstoke: Palgrave Macmillan, 2008).

Catherine Phuong, *The International Protection of Internally Displaced Persons* (Cambridge: Cambridge University Press, 2005).

UNHCR, *The State of the World's Refugees: Fifty Years of Humanitarian Action* (Oxford: Oxford University Press, 2000).

—— *The State ot the World's Refugees: Human Displacement in the New Millennium* (Oxford: Oxford University Press, 2006).

Aristide Zolberg, Astri Suhrke and Serio Aguayo, *Escape from Violence: Conflict and the Refugee Crisis in the Developing World* (New York: Oxford University Press, 1989).

Websites

Forced Migration: www.forcedmigration.org/
Internal Displacement Monitoring Centre: www.internal-displacement.org/
PRS Project: Towards solutions for protracted refugee situations: www.prsproject.org
Refugees International: www.refugeesinternational.org/
Reliefweb (administered by UN-OCHA): www.reliefweb.int
UNHCR: www.unhcr.org

Index

Addis Ababa Agreement (1972) 29
Afghan refugees 48, 61, 65–66, 69
Afghanistan: "refugee warriors"
    35–36, 37; regional conflict and
    prolonged refugee crises 35, 46,
    49; premature repatriation to 69,
    115; UNCHR–DPKO
    cooperation 88; IDPs 105, 108; as
    "failed and fragile state" 112;
    inter-agency collaboration for
    burden sharing 116
Africa: European colonies' demands
    for independence 22; liberation
    wars and post-independence
    conflict 25, 39, 111; UNHCR's
    re-orientation towards 25, 89;
    newly independent states added to
    international community 26, 100;
    UNHCR expansion of programs
    under Schnyder 27–29; emergence
    of refugee groups excluded from
    norms 28; regional legal norms
    relating to 28–29; conflicts and
    refugee movements in 1980s 31,
    32, 34, 35, 45–46, 101; returnees
    to newly independent former
    Portuguese territories 31;
    development planning initiatives
    38–39; push for resources and
    new approach in early 1980s
    39–40; states' failure to address
    prolonged conflicts in 1990s 55;
    states' restrictions on asylum in
    twenty-first century 61;
    international community's lack of
    support in late 1990s 94; China's

emerging interest in 97;
    protracted refugee situations in
    1970s and 1980s 111, *see also*
    ICARA; Organization of African
    Unity; *under names of regions*
African Union (AU) 86
Aga Khan, Sadruddin 26, 29–31
Agenda for Protection (2002) 62–63
agricultural projects, Guatemalan
    refugees in Mexico 43
Algeria 22, 23–25, 78, *113*
Algerian War of Independence 89
Amnesty International 30
Angola 22, 31, 49, 106
Annan, Kofi 51, 56, 58, 86
Annual Tripartite Consultations on
    Resettlement 117
anti-colonial struggles 35, 115
anti-terrorist laws 60
Argentina 29, 30
Armenia, scale of protracted refugee
    situation at end of 2004 *113*
Armenian refugees 8
Asia: European colonies' demands
    for independence 22; Cold War
    superpower rivalry for influence
    25; newly independent states
    added to international community
    26, 100; emergence of refugee
    groups excluded from norms 28;
    conflicts and refugee movements
    in 1980s 31, 32, 34, 45–46, 101;
    states' restrictions on asylum in
    first twenty-first century 61;
    UNHCR's expansion of activities
    into 89; host countries who have

GLOBAL INSTITUTIONS SERIES

NEW TITLE
The African Union
Challenges of globalization, security, and governance

Samuel M. Makinda, Murdoch University
F. Wafula Okumu, Institute for Security Studies

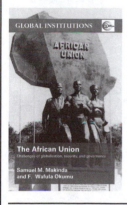

A comprehensive examination of the work of the African Union (AU), with special emphasis on its capacity to meet the challenges of building and sustaining governance institutions and security mechanisms.

Contents
Introduction 1. The Organization of African Unity and mutual preservation 2. The African Union: meeting the challenge of globalization 3. Governance, democracy, and the rule of law 4. Security and peace building 5. Knowledge and development 6. Challenges of globalization, security, and governance

October 2007: 216x138mm: 232pp
Hb: 978-0-415-40350-4: **£65.00**
Pb: 978-0-415-40349-8: **£14.99**

NEW TITLE
The European Union

Clive Archer, Manchester Metropolitan University

While there are many textbooks about the European Union (EU), Clive Archer covers the essential elements of the EU clearly and concisely, outlining the key debates and issues it faces today.

Contents
Introduction 1. The debate on the nature of the EU 2. A brief history of European integration 3. Institutions and processes 4. The EU's domestic policies 5. The EU's external activities 6. Where to now?

January 2008: 216x138mm: 200pp
Hb: 978-0-415-37012-7: **£65.00**
Pb: 978-0-415-37011-0: **£14.99**

Routledge
Taylor & Francis Group

To order any of these titles
Call: +44 (0) 1264 34 3071
Fax: +44 (0) 1264 34 3005
Email: book.orders@routledge.co.uk

For further information visit:
www.routledge.com/politics

GLOBAL INSTITUTIONS SERIES

NEW TITLE
The World Bank
From reconstruction to development to equity

Katherine Marshall, Georgetown University

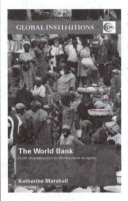

A concise and comprehensive overview of the World Bank's history, development, structure, functionality and activities.

Contents
Introduction 1. "In the catbird's seat": the World Bank and global development 2. How the World Bank has evolved in response to global events 3. Nuts and bolts: how the World Bank functions 4. Development partnerships and the World Bank 5. Grounding in realities: the World Bank at work 6. The World Bank and its critics 7. Looking ahead: challenges facing the World Bank 8. Conclusion: an ideal for the World Bank

February 2008: 216x138mm: 216pp
Hb: 978-0-415-38128-4: **£65.00**
Pb: 978-0-415-38132-1: **£14.99**

NEW TITLE
Contemporary Human Rights Ideas

Bertrand G. Ramcharan, Geneva Graduate Institute of International and Development Studies

This book provides an accessible introduction to the key human rights concepts, the current debates about human rights, strategies and institutions for taking forward the global implementation of human rights, and the core messages that need to be imparted to students and the public at large.

Contents
Introduction 1. History: shared heritage, common struggle 2. Human rights in the world community 3. International obligation 4. Universality 5. Equality 6. Democracy 7. Development 8. International cooperation and dialogue 9. Protection 10. Justice, remedy, and reparation 11. Conclusion

April 2008: 216x138mm: 224pp
Hb: 978-0-415-77456-7: **£65.00**
Pb: 978-0-415-77457-4: **£14.99**

Routledge
Taylor & Francis Group

To order any of these titles
Call: +44 (0) 1264 34 3071
Fax: +44 (0) 1264 34 3005
Email: book.orders@routledge.co.uk

For further information visit:
www.routledge.com/politics